INTELLECTUAL DEVELOPMENT: ANOTHER LOOK

Papers from
The ASCD Eighth Curriculum Research Institute

Edited by A. Harry Passow
Director of the Institute Staff
and
Robert R. Leeper
Editor, ASCD Publications

ASSOCIATION FOR SUPERVISION AND CURRICULUM DEVELOPMENT
1201 Sixteenth Street, N.W., Washington, D.C. 20036

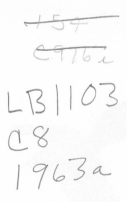
Copyright © *1964 by the*

ASSOCIATION FOR SUPERVISION AND CURRICULUM DEVELOPMENT
1201 Sixteenth Street, N.W., Washington, D.C. 20036

Price: $1.75

Library of Congress Catalog Card Number 64-8336

Contents

Foreword

FOR several years, published educational literature in the United States has been enriched periodically by papers presented at the Curriculum Research Institutes cosponsored by the Association for Supervision and Curriculum Development and the National Institute of Mental Health. The Association is indebted to its Research Commission for planning and executing these Institutes. Hundreds of interested persons have been privileged at the Institutes to rub elbows with and get ideas from persons pushing the frontiers of knowledge about human learning, the nature of knowledge, and effective instruction. The Association is particularly indebted to the scholars who have been willing to put their thoughts on paper and to participate in give-and-take discussions with Institute registrants following the presentations.

A much wider audience has, of course, been reached by the publication of the papers. Some of the previously published bulletins have become "best sellers"—and members of ASCD have come to expect something beyond the ordinary from this series. This particular publication, representing papers presented at the two sections of the Eighth Curriculum Research Institute, will undoubtedly add luster to the illustrious record already established. The authors, from their various perspectives, have taken "another look" at intellectual development which remains a central purpose of American education. Research which they have undertaken is reported; but of even greater significance are some proposals which they have made for curriculum and instruction—proposals which, if taken seriously and implemented, would require enormous changes in current programs and practices.

Those readers hoping for simple answers to instructional problems are likely to be disappointed with this publication. Those who wish to probe beyond simplicity will be stimulated to think, to question, to doubt; and perhaps even to begin some explorations of their own.

The National Institute of Mental Health, through Eli M. Bower, has made a significant contribution to the success of this Curriculum Research Institute through its aid in selecting consultants, staffing the Research Institute and making pertinent suggestions regarding its organization.

The Association especially recognizes the time and effort given to this publication by the editors, A. Harry Passow and Robert R. Leeper. Both of them have served ASCD and the education profession for years with distinction. We are grateful, again, for their dedication and their work.

September 1964
                                        Harold D. Drummond
                                        President, ASCD, 1964-65

Acknowledgments

FINAL editing of the manuscript and production of this booklet were the responsibility of Robert R. Leeper, Associate Secretary and Editor, ASCD Publications. Technical production was accomplished by Marjorie West, Editorial Aide, assisted by Teola Jones, Staff Assistant, under the general supervision of Ruth P. Ely, Editorial Associate.

Intellectual Development: Another Look

An Introduction

A. Harry Passow

CHILDREN ages two and three are being taught to read, write and spell. Algebraic and analytic geometry concepts form the basis for primary mathematics classes. Ideas reflecting such fundamental physical concepts as *force* and *motion* are studied by second and third graders. Anthropology is found in elementary school programs. A general moving down of units and topics traditionally taught in later grades into the curriculum of primary classes has become commonplace. Ideas about children's readiness for specific school experiences are being revised drastically. Bruner's hypothesis that "any subject can be taught effectively in some intellectually honest form to any child at any stage of development" has been interpreted by some program planners to mean that every subject should be taught as early as possible and at every stage of development. The role of the structure of the disciplines in curriculum planning is being studied.

Recent programs and proposals have stirred questions about the nature of children's intellectual development. Have genuine insights into how young children learn been uncovered? Have characteristics of intellectual development which warrant major curricular modifications been discovered? By possibly undervaluing the intellectual potential of younger children, has implied methodology been ignored? Are fundamental revisions in scope, sequence, and even organizing foci for curriculum required? As answers to questions such as these promise leads to deepening understanding, as the process-nature of inquiry and curiosity is clarified, the problems of choosing among curricular alternatives become more, not

1

less complex. Learning "capacity" of young children is one of the major criteria among several in determining appropriate curricular experiences.

Respect for the insights and opinions of mathematicians, physicists, linguists, geographers, anthropologists and others has sometimes outweighed knowledge about intellectual development and the nature of concept formation in choosing curricular content. The child development and learning theory bases for "new" curricular programs are often as unclear as they were for some earlier program reform efforts. Whether we are dealing with new knowledge about intellectual development or reinterpreting and applying earlier knowledge is not clear. What is apparent, certainly, is that exploration of the nature of intellectual development is proceeding at an accelerated pace. For the curriculum worker the time for a further look seems essential.

The six papers which follow were prepared for the two sections of the Eighth ASCD Curriculum Research Institute. Two deal with new views of intellectual development and cognitive structure; two deal with inquiry and curiosity in intellectual development and learning; and two with the reports of a physicist and a mathematician engaged in curriculum revision on the bases for their program proposals.

Intellectual Development—Some New Views

Millie Almy points out the need for teachers who thoroughly understand the way children think and how intelligence develops, especially during the period of early childhood. It is at this stage, she believes, that children "acquire and learn to process basic information that can either further or impede their later progress." Early childhood is indeed the critical point in the intellectual development of the child.

It is Piaget's ideas of intelligence as information-processing that Dr. Almy examines in detail, suggesting that eventually ideas concerning motivation and cognition, emotion and intellect will be integrated into a meaningful concept of the "whole child." Some of the newer views of intellectual development are contrasted with the traditional concepts. These include the idea of a "natural ordinal scale of intelligence" to help measure the degree to which different experiences accelerate the rate of intellectual development. In addition, the kind of perceptual and verbal experiences the child has in his early formative stages has a profound effect on his later intellectual ability.[1] By providing richer, more stimulating environments during the child's early development, a more rapid rate of intellectual development and a greater intellectual capacity may evolve.

To Dr. Almy, the possibilities of modifying educational environment

[1] For an extensive discussion of this view see: Benjamin S. Bloom. *Stability and Change in Human Characteristics.* New York: John Wiley & Sons, 1964. 237 p.

and procedures suggest what she calls a "renaissance of early childhood education." She identifies trends toward profitable curricular experimentation which reflect newer theories of intellectual development. These include the revival of earlier instructional systems, such as the Montessori materials and method, with more experimental insight than the old-fashioned operational testing. Another experimental direction involves cognitive analysis of specific curriculum content to enrich experiences. Still another trend involves the detailed analysis of a specific discipline into component parts which then are matched to the developing intellectual abilities of the children.

Dr. Almy questions whether programs which aim primarily at acceleration in a particular subject area actually benefit later intellectual development. She advises that far more should be done to understand and develop imagination in early childhood. For the educator, these views of intellectual development promise the opening of "new possibilities for influencing children's thinking, or guiding their encounters with the world in ways that will give them an increasingly better command over it." If this is done with insight and understanding, the consequence should be to free the child's intellect and to shape him into a more effective person.

In general, Millie Almy urges greater attention to understanding the encounters between children and their environment as these affect both the rate and the level of intellectual development. Effective teaching would capitalize on the child's ways of thinking at each level of intellectual development and at the same time challenge him to more adequate thinking. She suggests that Piaget's "clinical method" of questioning may also be used effectively by the teacher in assessing the child's level of thinking. Finally, Dr. Almy foresees the time when teachers, having a grasp of the basic methods and concepts of intellectual development, modify not only content but teaching methods as well, thus capitalizing on the concepts of readiness and individual differences.

Donald M. Johnson discusses cognitive structures and the development of intellectual processes. Beginning with an examination of the nature of concepts used in communication and in problem solving, Johnson discusses the ways in which these can be tested. A large part of education, he points out, consists of the acquisition of various kinds or systems of concepts, differing in abstractness and complexity. Dr. Johnson reminds us that conceptual structures, which have been neglected by educators, now attract renewed attention from curriculum developers. These cognitive structures are studied in several ways. Questions of superior programing for learning, the optimal sequence for presenting materials, the approaches which are most effective with particular students eventually will have to be worked out by teachers with their own materials and their own students. One of the likely gains, he suggests, from interest in programed learning is the finding that different sequences need to be tested. Possibly tests should explore, for instance, a policy of alternating between the specific and the general, between performance and verbalization, between multiple-choice and free-response formats. Alternating between various approaches might be better than spending equal time on either approach alone.

Johnson indicates that the virtue in "big generalizations and principles, the abstract cognitive structures" is their transferability to new situations. Supposedly they transfer better than the specific examples on which they are based. However, he speculates that if the teacher tries out three programs—one dealing with specific facts, a second largely with general principles, and a third alternating between the specific and the general—that the back-and-forth program would most likely be the most efficient. Optimum sequence for learning should probably start with specific elements at the proper level of difficulty, move as rapidly as possible to the general principles of higher level abstraction, return to more specifics and then to more general principles.

Teachers are warned not to imagine that because a problem has been solved once by a student, mastery is established. Johnson describes some of his own studies of learning and the development of cognitive processes, which suggest that the notion of "practice makes perfect" really requires modification and might be restated in terms of a certain kind of practice making a certain kind of perfection, for the nature and purpose are critical determinants.

Johnson proposes that "conceptual reorganizations achieved at advanced levels, as well as new facts, should be moved down to the elementary level as soon as possible." He bases this on the belief that some new conceptual systems are actually easier for the student to master if learned in a different framework and programed differently from the start. Selection and reorganization, rather than addition of information, are suggested as means for building a modern conception from the outset.

Curiosity, Exploration and Inquiry in Learning

The notion of curiosity as a "variable that apparently intervenes between the intellect and its manifestation" is the focus of the paper by Walter B. Waetjen. *Curiosity* has many definitions and varied usages in school situations. Dr. Waetjen explores a number of these and arrives at a description of curiosity as "one human dynamic that makes operational the intellect"—by leading to increased sensory data input and greater differentiation in the individual's perceptual field, the child's symbolic repertoire is broadened and altered and consequently his learning is facilitated.

The studies of curiosity in both laboratory and educational settings which Waetjen describes suggest that curiosity is a significant element in intellectual development. For example, one study indicated that children with a high level of curiosity seemed either to learn more or to retain more of what they had experienced. Curious children move out from a familiar position and attempt to make contact with aspects of the environment that are novel and more complex. The studies raise questions for the teacher as to optimum rates of introducing new stimuli into the teaching-learning situation or the issue of pacing as well as novelty of the stimuli. Insights from research on curiosity also have meaning for the teacher and his methodology. For instance, pre-questioning by the teacher apparently had the consequence of arousing the learner's curiosity and of disposing him toward acquisition of more information.

Waetjen discusses the conflicting views that (a) as an inherent human factor curiosity should be manifest at all levels of intellectual ability in varying degrees and (b) curiosity and intellectual ability are negatively correlated with low intelligence causing the individual to be less sensitive to those conflicting stimuli in the environment which are the genesis of curiosity. He suggests that the task with the retardate may be to bring stability and balance into his world of relative complexity and chaos.

The role of anxiety in curiosity is also examined and Waetjen indicates that the generalized finding is that psychological stress may result in preservation of a familiar behavioral and perceptual field so that curiosity is not aroused or stimulated. Further, the degree to which the individual is receptive to new or strange situations is influenced by the security nourished by his parents.

Finally, Waetjen summarizes research evidence concerning personality correlates and curiosity. He suggests that individual personality styles may account for preferences for simplicity, order and organization on the one hand or complexity, ambiguity and relative disorder on the other. It is the "self as data processor" that determines how the input data related to curiosity is actually acted on by the organism.

J. Richard Suchman probes the child and the inquiry process, suggesting the ability to inquire as a necessary condition for the independence and autonomy of learning. Beyond this, inquiry is a fundamental form of learning. In examining the nature of inquiry Suchman explores two basic processes: assimilation, taking in and incorporating perceptions in terms of knowledge and understanding; and accommodation, reshaping and reorganizing conceptual structures to fit and account for events as perceived. Both assimilation and accommodation are involved in the inquiry process, for the individual is faced with a discrepant event which he must analyze and which he must restructure to fit the observed conditions. Thus, inquiry to Suchman is a fundamental learning process under the autonomous control of the learner, a process which promotes conceptual growth.

The development of thinking from the intuitive and concrete to the analytic and abstract is particularly apparent in the inquiry process. Suchman relates inquiry to cognitive styles (e.g., highly-analytical thinking styles compared with rational or low-analytical styles) and suggests that the process of inquiry has a large "creative component." Viewing inquiry as basic to all intellectual activity, Suchman has experimented with the teaching of strategies and tactics of inquiry, using question-and-answer investigation as the means for structuring the sessions. In one study, Suchman found that conceptual growth was as vigorous through the inquiry approach as with the more traditional didactic methods. He argues that the basic test of inquiry training would be the degree to which its skills can be transferred to problems in other content areas: if inquiry can be developed and strengthened through these exercises and through the deliberate shaping of strategies and techniques, then training would have wide-ranging applicability.

The most significant outcome of inquiry training, Suchman observes, is that growth of autonomy of the learner seems important for both motivation and conceptual growth. The preliminary findings encourage Suchman to propose an "inquiry-centered curriculum" in which "learning would always be in connection with moving from concrete events toward the construction of an explanatory model." Such a curriculum, he believes, would have at least four outcomes: It would develop and strengthen the inquiry process itself, enhance the self-image of the pupil as autonomous learner, provide greater depth of understanding of the principles and concepts within the disciplines relevant to the problems and put the process and products of inquiry into a proper balance. In strengthening the inquiry process, cognitive functions would be developed which would nurture the learner's thinking so as to produce new concepts.

Although he uses science content, Suchman does not propose that inquiry training be adapted to science teaching only; rather it is a tool for teaching the basic cognitive skills of reasoning and the formulating and testing of hypotheses. In perceiving the process as a basic one in cognition, Suchman assumes its general applicability regardless of the disciplinary content. The focus on the process has direct application for teaching method.

Bases for Two Curriculum Revision Programs

Physicist Robert Karplus discusses the Science Curriculum Improvement Study in terms of its contribution to the general education of students. Stressing his belief that the conceptual structure of science is something entirely different from the conceptual structure of common sense, he sees the function of education as guiding a child's development by providing experiences that will serve as a base for abstractions, as a key to the perception of meaningful phenomena, and a force integrating inferences into lasting, meaningful generalizations. For Karplus the starting point for scientific endeavor is an observation interpreted in the light of "the scientific point of view" or the synthesis of past experience. Scientific truth is not absolute and permanent but rather in accordance with the facts as currently known. The implication is that instruction should aim to give students sufficient knowledge and experience to understand other people's scientific work, even though they themselves do not become scientists. It is the quality of what he calls "scientific literacy" that is or should be the major objective of the science curriculum.

Karplus contends that the full value of the "new" secondary school science program can be realized only when the elementary science curriculum builds the proper foundation for the child's own investigations. With such a background, it is quite likely that secondary school courses would have to be modified even further. He suggests that the elementary program should consist to a large extent of opportunities for direct experiences for children with considerable teacher guidance and discussion, so that each lesson establishes or reinforces an abstract concept. As for the conceptual structure, creating a context for a new experience facilitates its rational assimilation in relation to other experiences. The purposes of proposals for developing scientific literacy among younger children stem from Karplus' ideas about the nature of science and the nature of the learning process. His program would attempt to teach pupils to look at natural phenomena from the scientific point of view, developing verbal labels to enable them to discriminate between concepts. This, he believes, young children are capable of doing efficiently and effectively.

The heavy reliance on textbooks and other secondary sources of information instead of the kind of direct experiences that aim at developing the child's "common sense rationality" has the effect of building resentment against science or building an abstract structure that readily atrophies. Karplus would place far greater stress on nurturing in each pupil a strong feeling of the integrity of his own observations, for science is impossible without this attitude. The starting point of all scientific endeavor is observation. Of course, Karplus does not advocate that the pupil learn only from his own observations. Rather, he suggests that "to be able to use information obtained by others, the individual must have a conceptual structure and a means of communication that enable him to interpret the information as though he had obtained it himself." It is this understanding that he labels scientific literacy.

Patrick Suppes discusses the formation of mathematical concepts in primary grade children as the basis of program planning. Contrasting programs emphasizing understanding concepts and those perfecting rote skills, Suppes suggests that describing the latter as essentially "bad" and the former as basically "good" represents too simple and meaningless a characterization. Instead, he advises greater attention to the questions of transfer of concepts through various kinds of curriculum and to specification of behaviors involved in understanding. Better formulation and testing of workable hypotheses to clarify the efficacy of "the discovery method of teaching" urged by proponents of newer mathematics programs, are also suggested.

Suppes and his colleagues have attempted to apply a stimulus sampling learning theory to experiments dealing with the mathematical concept formation in young children. Six such experiments are described, in which simple theoretical notions are used as the basis for introducing the child to arithmetic concepts and operations. From these studies as well as from related research, Suppes sets forth some tentative but promising conclusions. These have to do with the formation of mathematical concepts (generally an all-or-none process although there are deviations); the increased efficiency of learning related to the conditions of error correction (greater efficiency with overt correction in presence of stimulus); the relative ineffectiveness of incidental learning (tends not to be an effective method for learning the underlying concepts); contiguity of response as reinforcement in improving learning; the effects of learning related concepts on the amount of overall transfer (positive or negative transfer between specific sub-concepts may be greater); and the improvement of transfer when multi-stimuli exist. Suppes points out that some of these tentative conclusions disagree with accepted findings about adult learning behavior. For this reason, he sees the need for more systematic analysis of the differences between learning patterns of young children and of adults.

Finally, Suppes reports briefly on some ongoing work aimed at introducing the more able elementary school pupil to mathematical content and methods at a completely exacting level which is simple enough in presentation and content to permit relatively easy comprehension. These experiments are designed to test the underlying rationale of some of the newer mathematics programs on young children. Can young children undertake the kinds of deductive proof basic to modern mathematics? Also, are skills in analysis and reasoning derived from mathematics operations transferable to other subject areas?

In a related paper, Suppes states his belief that the most significant improvements in subject-matter learning will be the consequence of intensive study of individual differences along dimensions presently ignored:

"The optimum sequencing of curriculum materials, the analysis of subject matter so as to present it in steps of the proper size, etc., are not nearly so important elements in learning as the single one of individual accommodation." [2] Concentration on individual differences in learning is presently going forward in a computer-based laboratory which facilitates the applications of learning theory to the school curriculum by bridging the gap between research on learning and curriculum development. The computer-based laboratory collects and handles large quantities of behavioral data in ways that were not possible previously.

Some Common Foci and Ideas

These six papers sample some of the theory and research dealing with intellectual development, stating implications for the selection and organization of learning opportunities for children. They point up the need for analyzing the structure of disciplines but in terms of what is known about concept formation and the fundamental development of mental abilities. The consequence in mathematics and science programs, for example, has been the reassessment of the ability of children to use symbolism in meaningful operations and manipulate relatively complex structures. Other foci deal with ideas about readiness, concept formation, abstraction and generalization, transfer and motivation.

While the ideas concerning readiness and the development of cognitive processes have caused supporters of some new programs to declare that the limits of learning have been grossly underestimated, they have caused others to question whether specific content should be placed earlier. Feasibility alone is not a sufficient criterion for determination of experiences for children. As Fred Tyler puts it:

Just the fact that children can learn this or that does not by itself mean that we, therefore, must require them to do so at some age or in some early grade. A whole network of related philosophical, sociological, psychological, and educational questions must be tackled before we can come to a practical judgment as expressed in questions like: Why should we introduce the material? What is the intended purpose? Is the objective feasible? [3]

Considerable attention has been given to understanding the psychological dimensions of readiness for particular experiences. Ausubel, for instance, sees the concept of readiness as the relationship between the adequacy of capacity and the demands of a given learning task with no specification for how this capacity is achieved. On the other hand,

[2] Patrick Suppes. "Modern Learning Theory and the Elementary School Curriculum." *American Educational Research Journal* 1: 82; March 1964.

[3] Fred Tyler. "Issues Related to Readiness to Learn." In *Theories of Learning and Instruction*, 63rd Yearbook of the National Society for the Study of Education, Part I. Chicago: University of Chicago Press, 1964. p. 238-39.

maturation encompasses growth in capacity that takes place without specific practice or experience. Maturation and learning are two factors that contribute to and determine the child's readiness to cope with a new experience. Pedagogically, Ausubel contends, this concept of readiness implies two conditions: (a) teaching methods should take account of general developmental changes in cognitive functioning and (b) the curriculum should be organized sequentially to foster pupils' readiness for each new unit after mastery of the previous unit. Thus, flat statements about readiness of individuals or age-groups have little meaning since "readiness is always relative to a particular subject matter, topic, level of difficulty and method of teaching." [4]

There are disagreements, however, about measuring readiness for specific instructional purposes. Tyler points out that the pupil may have cognitive readiness and yet be deficient in certain aspects of non-cognitive readiness. Instruction will not move smoothly if the educator waits for readiness to come from passage of time more than if he acts as if it were present at any age. What researchers such as Tyler say to the curriculum planner is that he "must provide for, produce or build tenable cognitive and non-cognitive readiness" if he is to contribute directly and deliberately to the improvement of teaching and learning. [5]

From the evidence amassed concerning the intellectual development of children, Hunt concludes that leaving children alone while they "mature" has had unfortunate consequences. The challenge he poses is one of finding

. . . ways to govern the encounters that children have with their environments, especially during the early years of their development, to achieve a substantially faster rate of intellectual development and a substantially higher adult level of intellectual capacity. Moreover, inasmuch as the optimum rate of intellectual development would mean also self-directing interest and curiosity and genuine pleasure in intellectual activity, promoting intellectual development need imply nothing like the grim urgency which has been associated with "pushing" children. [6]

The current interest in making schools more intellectually exciting can be described, at least in part, as an effort to enhance and capitalize on insights derived from studies of intellectual development. Observing the state of flux of the field, Cronbach [7] noted that, "Old dogmas are lying in the dust or tottering on their bases. Over-simple theories are being re-

[4] David P. Ausubel. *The Psychology of Meaningful Verbal Learning.* New York: Grune & Stratton, 1963. p. 111-12.

[5] Fred Tyler, *op. cit.,* p. 239.

[6] J. McV. Hunt. *Intelligence and Experience.* New York: Ronald Press, 1961. p. 363.

[7] Lee J. Cronbach. "The Psychological Background for Curriculum Experimentation." In *Modern Viewpoints in the Curriculum.* Paul C. Rosenbloom, editor. New York: McGraw-Hill Book Co., 1964. p. 34.

modeled to take disturbing findings and insights into account." Lest old dogmas be replaced by new ones on equally shaky bases, educators and curriculum reformers need to understand and take into account the new insights, the revised interpretations, the deeper understandings of the dimensions of intellectual development. A further look is timely and these six papers are an attempt to do this.

New Views on
Intellectual Development
in Early Childhood Education

Millie Almy

AMERICANS, according to anthropologists, are committed to change, to the notion that what is new, or at least different, is probably better. The pendulum of popular interest swings in wide arcs as people espouse first one, then another idea.

Psychologists and educators like their contemporaries are pendulum prone, though they do not always swing in the same direction at the same time. During the years I have spent as an educator and developmental psychologist I have noted three major swings beginning with the habit training and behavior inventories of the 'thirties. Next came a considerable preoccupation with the social and emotional aspects of development and, to a lesser extent, concern with the personal and subjective aspects of child behavior. Now interest centers on the intellectual aspects of development.

Concern with the cognitive or, as it is often phrased, with concept formation, is widely manifest in educational circles these days. Visit one kindergarten in which the children are playing with blocks, another in which a painting of a dinosaur is the big attraction, one in which the children are coloring flags for Washington's Birthday, or even one in which the curriculum is built around reading readiness workbooks. Each of the teachers will likely tell you his program is designed to build concepts. "Readiness" is no longer a fashionable term.

To catch up with psychological jargon is simple. Yet the challenge to education, implicit in emerging theories of intellectual development, cannot be met by mere lip service. It will demand teachers who are well informed and thoughtful, and who understand as much about the ways children think as they do about the subjects they teach. Furthermore, the demands on early childhood education will be at least as great, perhaps greater, than for any other level of education. For it is at that level that children acquire and learn to process basic information that can either further or impede their later progress, that may indeed either enhance or stultify their intellectual powers.

Intelligence as Information Processing

Several popular definitions of intelligence have been stated, such as "the capacity to profit from experience," or even, "that which the intelligence test tests." Such statements imply something more global and more fixed than does the presently emerging view that intelligence is "the variety of ways an individual has available for processing or organizing incoming information." Such a view allows for a more adequate analysis of the varieties of thinking that underlie intelligent behavior, and of the role that experience plays in their development.

So many psychologists have contributed to this view of intelligence as information processing that one hesitates to begin to name them, although Guilford, Osgood, Hebb, and Bruner come immediately to mind. None of these has been so concerned with the *development* of these processes as has Piaget, although most of his theoretical formulations have been put in other terms. Since Piaget himself has speculated that information theory and game theory might provide a needed common language for those interested in various aspects of child development, it is not inappropriate for me to translate some of his concepts into these terms. In so doing I shall aim for common clarity with an emphasis on what I believe to be the implications of his theory rather than attempting to elucidate the theory precisely. Those who have struggled with Piaget's theory will I hope bear with me. Those who are less familiar will perhaps be grateful for an oversimplification. As someone has said, Piaget's writing is often difficult, perhaps because he does not wish to obscure the great darkness of his subject.

Essentially the view of intelligence that I shall present says that intelligence, rather than being fixed by genetic factors at birth, emerges as it is nurtured. Each stage of development carries with it possibilities for the acquisition of new abilities, new ways of processing information. Unless each of these abilities is sufficiently exercised as it emerges, it will not develop fully and it will contribute little if at all to the demands of the next stage.

Piaget's theory encompasses the development of information processing from the infant's earliest sucking, looking and eventual reaching and grasping, to the adolescent's ability to manipulate logical propositions mentally. It is a theory wherein the person's grasp of the ideas encountered in algebra and geometry, chemistry and physics represents the top level of a hierarchy of experiences beginning at birth. Along one dimension the person has moved from a completely subjective view of the world, to one that is increasingly objective. On another dimension, the concrete-abstract, he has moved from "a world of things present to a world of things possible."

The models Piaget has chosen to represent thought processes are the "operations" of logic and mathematics. Psychologists and educators who know Piaget only from such early volumes as *Language and Thought* (1924a), or *Judgment and Reasoning* (1924b) may be shocked to find the discursive musings of the children in those volumes replaced in the *Growth of Logical Thinking* (1955) with experiments in which the child manipulates materials and both his actions and his comments are summarized in statements written in symbolic logic. We are not accustomed to thinking of children's thoughts in terms of P's and Q's, implications, and disjunctions. This child seems a different child, largely because Piaget and his collaborator, Inhelder, focus so exclusively on the concrete-abstract dimension of his thought, making reference to the subjective-objective dimension only to explain or clarify difficulties in the other dimension.

The present theory, then, takes explicit account only of the kind of thought that is clearly reality adjusted. This theory deals primarily with the ways the person gains factual knowledge and the ways he orders facts, but not with the ways he feels about or values them.

Patterns of Action

Perhaps we can also say that the theory applies best in those instances in which the developing child's basic needs for emotional security are being adequately met. Piaget acknowledges the interaction between emotion and intellect, but his is not a dynamic theory in the usual sense. Wolff (1960), in a comparison of the developmental psychologies of Freud and Piaget, has pointed out that Piaget is not concerned with long-range forces or drives corresponding to physiologic or homeostatic imbalances, but rather with short-range forces involving a need to function. Similarly, Bruner (1959) has indicated that Piaget's theory of cognition will not be complete until he integrates into it the goals for which people strive. J. McV. Hunt (1961) on the other hand has suggested that Piaget's notions about the development of cognition can appropriately be integrated into emerging theories of motivation. Piaget's children, like Berlyne's rats and Harlow's monkeys, are intrinsically curious and active. They respond to the strange, the unfamiliar and the incongruous in ways consonant with current models of cognitive dissonance, incongruity or imbalance. Piaget, himself (Tanner and Inhelder, 1960), has suggested that such diverse views on affective and personality development as those held by psychoanalysts such as Erikson, and Bowlby, and the anthropologist, Margaret Mead, could be synthesized with his (Piaget's) theory of intellectual development. Such a synthesis would involve the idea that the child acts on information derived from interpersonal situations and involving emotions and feelings in much the same way that he handles information conveyed from physical or impersonal sources. In either case the strategy is to obtain maximum information or gratification with minimum expenditure of cognitive or psychic pain.

Whether or not Piaget's formulations figure extensively in the emerging theories of psychology, it seems likely that motivation and cognition, emotion and intellect will eventually receive less disparate treatment than in the past. Perhaps when this happens we can at last put some specific meanings into the slippery concept of the "whole child," long used so glibly by so many educators.

For an elucidation of Piaget's views, however, it seems most feasible to look at the cognitive child, thinking of him as a youngster brought up by parents who are reasonably loving, who have some appreciation for his growing powers, and who have thoughtfully provided him with brothers and sisters with whom he is only moderately rivalrous. We shall consider him to be motivated at least as much by his own pleasure in functioning, his own satisfaction in solving problems or resolving contradictions as he is by his mother's smiles and pats, his father's praise, or the "goods" his teacher may write on his paper.

This child is born with receptors that bring him information, initially meaningless, about the sights, the sounds, the tastes of the world around him. Similarly he is endowed with motor equipment that soon enables him not only to focus visually but even to turn his head toward an object, a face, a sound. Gradually his hands follow the lead of his eyes, and impressions from visual and auditory modalities are coordinated with tactual information.

From the standpoint of developing intelligence, he may be regarded as storing information in *patterns of action*. Piaget calls these sensorimotor schemata, and sees them increasing in complexity and relatedness throughout the first eighteen months or so of life. The infant grasps the rattle that is thrust in front of him and brings it to his mouth. Vary the position of the rattle, place it further from his reach, change its size and its shape and the infant, finding that his original pattern is not adequate, varies it, in Piaget's terms, accommodating himself to it. In the

15

process, the action patterns or schemata are modified. Again, in Piaget's terms, the information from the environment is assimilated into the schemata. Through an intricate series of such accommodations and assimilations the child becomes increasingly facile at manipulating his world, and the world in a sense becomes increasingly predictable for him. Indeed one of the landmarks of the period comes when the child's ability to apprehend an object, presumably through having explored it visually and manipulatively in a variety of settings, enables him to recognize it even after it has momentarily disappeared from view. This is the beginning of the ability to "conserve," to comprehend the essential stability or invariance of many aspects of the surrounding environment,

For a considerable part of the infancy period the child's intelligence reveals itself primarily in what he does to the things he encounters. There is relatively little evidence of planning or anticipating. Yet as his actions become better and better adapted, as his world is consequently enlarged, as he attempts more and more to imitate its aspects, it appears that he no longer needs to operate on it so directly. He remembers previous actions and he applies them mentally. Thus he enters into what Piaget has called representative intelligence. By now he has to some extent accommodated his own vocal productions to those he has heard around him and is beginning to assimilate a vocabulary. He has labels for some of his own actions. Such labels, and the ability to acquire more, tremendously speed up the rate at which he can store information and of course also speed up the process of information retrieval.

Let us pause at this point, marking the place where human intelligence departs from simian, and note three important aspects of the theory described thus far.

First, this is more than a maturation theory. The increasing complexity and adaptibility of the action patterns are dependent, not only on growth, but on the child's opportunities *to act on* something.

Second, what a child assimilates, what gets incorporated into the repertoire of action patterns in part depends on the patterns he already has available. Mothers recognize this when they match their expectations for independent spoon feeding to the way the baby grabs for the spoon. Similarly, parental attempts to teach baby a new word are usually contingent on the sounds he is already making, and most successful when the match between the baby's repertoire and the new syllables is fairly close.

Third, new patterns do not emerge full-blown and perfect. They are spontaneously practiced as the child plays in his crib, his pen, his bath. You have heard infants babbling a repertoire of sounds that are almost but not quite English, and the slightly older child putting himself to sleep going over all the words he knows.

In summary, the infant does not maximize his intellective power unless he is exposed to a rather wide variety of stimuli, unless the opportunities presented by these stimuli are relatively well matched by the complexity of the action patterns the child already has available, and unless these opportunities are followed by much time for spontaneous play.

Using Labels for Experience

Once he has begun to use language, the infant, now a toddler, enters into a new stage of development, during which his ways of thinking become progressively more like those of the adult. Partly, this is a result of the child's becoming more and more adept at acquiring labels for experience, and also at matching new experiences to already available labels, that is, at forming concepts. Partly this progress comes from an increasing ability to isolate particular aspects of experience and to deal with the relationships between those aspects mentally rather than directly.

The toddler who tries the "kitty" label on all small furry creatures gradually takes note of the long ears and short tails of some of them and applies a new label. He has created a new category or schema for storing or classifying information. What labels do two- or three-year-olds attach to the first white rat, the first guinea pig or hamster they encounter? Note that their classification is concrete in that they appear to match the unknown instance against their recollection of other specific instances of kitty or bunny. And it appears that, for a considerable time, "animal" is a second name applicable to cats, rabbits, guinea pigs, and so on, rather than an over-arching category into which many instances can be put.

Just as the young child acquires labels for the objects in the environment, so he also learns to label their properties and attributes. He notes color, shapes, sizes, textures, sounds, movement tendencies and so on; but the concepts of properties apart from the objects implied in words like big and small, light and heavy, up and down, behind, beside and before are complicated by the child's tendency to judge them more from their reference to himself than their reference to each other. Have you ever tried to *explain* a procedure for lining up to take turns on a slide to a group of young three-year-olds or inexperienced four-year-olds? Initially, Johnny's acceptance of the idea that placing himself always behind Dick and in front of Tom will bring his turn in orderly fashion is much more a matter of faith in the adult making the arrangement than in his own understanding of it.

Gradually, however, as the child checks his view of this and other situations with their actual outcomes, he modifies his thinking to obtain a better fit with outer reality. While at an earlier period he accommodated his actions to the size and shape of the objects he encountered, now he is accommodating thought patterns to more and more dimensions of his experience. He not only assimilates the new information into already established categories but creates new categories and gradually develops greater flexibility in categorizing.

The way young children deal with the problem of objects that float and objects that sink is illustrative. Although we might assume that young children with a moderate amount of experience with water play could predict adequately whether or not certain familiar objects placed in water would sink or float, many of them are surprisingly inaccurate. They have some notions about the objects but not about the objects in the water. We can question them about why they think a particular object will behave as they have predicted, seeking not for a scientific explanation but rather for an indication of which aspects of the objects they were attending. The young children (threes and fours) note whether the objects are large or small, or simply observe that an object goes up or down or that it "has to." As they grow older, the weight dimension of the objects is noted. The old notion that big objects float and little objects sink no longer accommodates adequately to the incoming information. The big-little schemata is gradually transformed into a fourfold categorization involving big-heavy and big-light objects as contrasted with little-heavy and little-light objects. Still later a notion of relative weight is assimilated into the thought pattern.

Arrival at the ability to deal simultaneously with relationships between two aspects of an object is preceded by the development of a new kind of conservation. Just as the child's encounters with his environment in the sensorimotor period led him to the discovery of the constancy of objects, so in the period of "concrete operations" he comes to the discovery of the invariance, or constancy, of an increasing number of *aspects* of objects. From these discoveries he eventually arrives at a grasp of the mathematical idea that quantity is not changed when a set of objects is partitioned into subgroups and the physical idea that mass or substance does not change when the shape or appearance of an object is transferred. Piaget's tests for demonstrating whether or not a child has achieved this kind of conservation are fairly well known. One of them involves confronting the child with a ball of clay that is pulled out or flattened, or broken in small pieces, and testing to find out whether he thinks the amount of clay changes as its appearance changes. Another test involves establishing with the child the identity in number of two rows of objects—say cubes—then bunching one row together, or spreading it apart to test whether the child thinks quantity changes with change in configuration. Another test involves establishing identity between two amounts of liquid and then testing to see whether the child retains that identity when he sees the liquid in one vessel poured into another of different shape.

It is only recently that these tests have been tried with American children. To a considerable extent Piaget's findings have been verified. In a study in which I am currently involved we tested some 330 children in kindergarten, first and second grade. In a middle-class school only nine percent of kindergarteners were able to conserve a number of blocks and a given amount of liquid. At first grade this percent rose to 32 and at second grade to 48. This gives some idea of the gradualness of the transition. In a lower-class school the trends were similar but the transition was much less rapid and only 23 percent of the second graders in this school were able to conserve consistently.

More important than the mere fact of transition is the question of its meaning. To what extent is the ability to conserve related to or facilitating of the child's thinking in other areas?

The practical dilemma of the child who is not yet conserving can be illustrated by the case of the youngster who had been asked to count five bottles by her teacher when a visitor arrived. The visitor suggested that the counting continue. The child had counted the bottles going from left to right. When the teacher asked her to repeat the process she pointed to the right hand bottle. The child was baffled, could not do it, finally in desperation turned to the left hand bottle, named it "one," the next "two," and so on. Then the teacher further confused her by saying, "Now put the five away." This child had no notion of number as a concept apart from specific objects.

Our own research indicates that children who conserve early are also advanced on other maturity measures including a reading readiness test. They also do better on a test that purports to be a test of logical abilities, the Stencil Design Test. Further analysis of our data may shed additional light on the nature of these and other relationships. Longitudinal study of the kindergarten children is designed to indicate whether early conservers have any marked advantages over other children.

Piaget associates arrival at the ability to conserve amount or quantity with the ability to perform a variety of logical operations heretofore impossible. These include not only the addition and subtraction of mathematics but also the operations involved in constructing logical classes. While the child, as we have suggested, has long been categorizing his experience so that he has an awareness of objects belonging together, or a common general name adhering to a large number of instances, it is only now that he begins to be able to hold a large category constant while he manipulates subcategories. Thus he recognizes that such a general class as say "animal," can be subdivided, for example, into land

19

animals and sea animals, and that the totality of land animals will exceed that of either the land or the sea animals. Similarly he can conceive the same general class "animal" as made up of vertebrates and invertebrates.

Increasing flexibility also appears in the child's ability to comprehend *mentally* certain other relationships. For example, knowing that John is taller than Jim, but shorter than George, he can arrive at the notion that Jim is the shortest or George the tallest without needing to see all three together. In somewhat similar fashion he can grasp the reciprocal nature of a left-hand relationship, understanding that a person who is a foreigner in one country is also a native in another, and so on.

Up to this point concrete operations, according to the Piaget theory, have been in formation. Beyond this, they are applied to more and more areas of experience. The turning point comes for most children around the ages of seven or eight years. Consequently, it is appropriate to regard the early childhood years, encompassing nursery school, kindergarten, first and second grades, as the years when thought is in transition between sensorimotor and concrete operations.

In other words, there is a hierarchy from the period when the sensorimotor schemata become integrated with the first words, through the period of early childhood when so much basic information is being stored and classified, and when new possibilities for classification develop so rapidly, into the period of middle and later childhood when concrete operational thinking facilitates a different grasp of reality, and finally to the time when formal operational thinking opens up the realm of possibility, and thinking can deal effectively in relationships among abstractions.

Now it is appropriate to review the principles discussed earlier when we considered the transition from infancy to toddlerhood.

First, *more than maturation is involved.* The increasing complexity and adaptability of the child's thought are contingent on his opportunities to think about something, to have appropriate new experiences.

Second, *what a child assimilates, what gets incorporated into his repertoire of thought processes, what challenges him to reorganize or reclassify information is in part dependent on the processes and the systems he already has available.* As one experimenter has put it, "The possibility of inducing a cognitive reorganization depends on the child's already available schemata. If he already has a structure which approaches the given notion the probability of the desired reorganization is high, whereas if he is still far from the notion the chances are small. . . ." (Smedslund, 1961).

Third, *abstract patterns of thinking, like concrete patterns, do not emerge full-blown but are rather the product of a series of encounters with ideas in which the child's thought has accommodated itself to new*

20

relationships, and the ability to comprehend these has been somewhat assimilated into the repertoire of thought processes so that they can be applied more and more widely.

Views of Intellectual Development

How do these views of intellectual development differ from those that have been more generally held?

They would substitute for the psychometric notions of an intelligence sufficiently fixed by heredity so that a child's position relative to his peers should remain constant throughout the period of development, the notion of a *natural ordinal* scale of intelligence. The position a child had reached on such a scale would indicate the intellectual progress he had already made, but prediction of development from that point forward would have to be predicated on knowledge of the experiences in store for him.

Implicit in such a notion is the possibility of some degree of acceleration of the rate of intellectual development. If the existence of a natural ordinal scale can be established, then the way is open to measure the effects of varying kinds of experience on the rate of transition from one point on the scale to the next.

It may well be that interactions between perceptual and verbal experience, in the period when concepts are being formed, have considerable to do with the kind of general intellective ability the child displays later on. Further evidence on this may come from studies of enrichment for culturally deprived children whose general intellective ability is so often extremely low. These youngsters at the preschool level do not appear so much to lack perceptual experience as verbal labels to apply to it. On the basis of my own observations, I think it likely when nursery school teachers make a deliberate effort to help the child with such labeling, conceptualization may speed up considerably.

Hunt (p. 363) has described [1] the possibilities in the new views on intellectual development:

. . . It might be feasible to discover ways to govern the encounters that children have with their environments, especially during the early days of their development, to achieve a substantially faster rate of intellectual development and a substantially higher intellectual capacity. Moreover, inasmuch as the optimum rate of intellectual development would mean also self-directing interest and curiosity and genuine pleasure in intellectual activity, promoting intellectual development properly need imply nothing like the grim urgency which has been associated with "pushing" children. Furthermore, these proce-

---

[1] J. McV. Hunt. *Intelligence and Experience.* New York: The Ronald Press Co., 1961. p. 363. Copyright © 1961 The Ronald Press Company.

dures, insofar as they tended to maximize each child's potential for intellectual development would not decrease individual differences in intellectual capacity as assessed by tests but would increase them.

Hunt goes on to indicate that to discover effective ways of governing children's environmental encounters would require a tremendous amount of research, and that once those were found the task of changing child rearing practices and educational procedures would be Herculean.

Research that can throw light on some of the questions raised by the new theories is already under way. Numerous attempts to change educational procedures at the first and second grade levels, and to a lesser extent in kindergarten and nursery school, are in progress. If interest in the early childhood years continues, and if educational experimentation at that level involves sufficient awareness of the repercussions it may have on the development of children's thinking at later levels, future historians may refer to the '60's as the beginning of the renaissance of early childhood education. Nursery and kindergarten education will emerge from the doldrums of the past ten or fifteen years and assume an importance equal to or perhaps even greater than first and second grades. In any event, it seems clear that education in the early childhood years can become more fruitful than is often the case at the present time.

Trends in Experimentation

It may be profitable to examine present curricular experimentation in early childhood in the light of the theory of intellectual development presented here. Unfortunately, almost none of the experimentation familiar to me includes provision for long term follow-up, or adequate study of comparable children who were not involved in the experimental programs. Without such provision, present experimentation will contribute little to the understanding of intellectual development.

One trend in experimentation is to revive the use of an earlier system of instruction. The widespread interest in Montessori materials and methods is perhaps the best illustration. In many respects Montessori's ideas run parallel to those of Piaget. But questions of whether the materials provide sufficient diversity for adequate concept formation, whether imagination is given free enough rein, and whether sufficient attention is given to social and interpersonal concepts all need investigation.

A second trend, and one that seems very promising in some of its manifestations, involves making a cognitive analysis of the content of a given curriculum. On the basis of such analysis enriching opportunities are provided. The teacher's customary ways of working with the children do not change, but the intellectual content of the experiences does change. How successful such ventures are seems to depend on the teacher's abilities to infer from the children's comments and other behavior the level of their understanding. For example in a program for so-called socially disadvantaged four-year-olds, a teacher, who was attempting to show some of the children the possibilities in block building, discovered that the word "wall" had no meaning for them. Moving from the block construction to the wall of the room she asked them to tell her what this was. They said, "paint." In somewhat similar fashion she discovered that for them "animal" was not even a second name for a horse, let alone a category in which horse might be put. Similarly a parakeet was not a bird. When teachers become aware of the hierarchy of experiences that are involved in concept formation, they are not so inclined to think that a child has a concept because he has been exposed to some examples of it. They learn to provide opportunities for him to demonstrate his understanding. They learn to use open-ended questions to find out where a child is in his thinking, and to reserve the more pointed, leading questions for the instances in which they can assume his understanding and want to reinforce it by having him make a correct response.

Another trend in curriculum experimentation involves attempts to break down specific disciplines into their component parts, and to match the learning of these to the developing intellectual abilities of the children. An especially happy example of this, according to reports, is the mathematics curriculum devised by Dienes in England. He has designed a set of materials, blocks of varying kinds, abacuses and so on, with which children in the infant school (kindergarteners and first graders in our system) can teach themselves the basic mathematical concepts. Teach themselves, that is, *provided* they have a teacher who understands how children think. Such a teacher never tells the child that he is right or wrong, but does provide him apparatus that enables him to make his own discoveries and to correct his own mistakes. In such situations the child moves at his own pace and is rewarded by his increasing mastery. This is exactly what Piaget's theory suggests should happen and appears to be an ideal way to enhance intellectual power.

In this country current experimentation involves not only mathematics and reading, but science, economics, linguistics and foreign languages. Fortunately, as far as I know, no one has attempted to experiment in all these areas at the same time, with the same children. Yet the fact that there are so many different approaches to young children in so many different areas of the curriculum raises some important questions so far as the nature of intellectual development is concerned.

The problem is illustrated by the current experimentation in elementary science carried on by Robert Karplus. Karplus, who is himself a physicist, is attempting to teach first graders some of the vocabulary and the concepts that are basic to modern science. In doing this he has children identify and describe objects and their properties, sort and match them on the basis of those properties, count them, measure them and so on. Clearly these activities involve mathematics, reading and language as well as science. Clearly some of them are as appropriate to kindergarten as to first grade, and all of them seem to have at least as much to do with the development of logical thinking as with science.

If the early childhood period is to capitalize more effectively on the learning and thinking propensities of children, more attention needs to be given to the question of which learnings are basic to later intellectual understanding in a particular area of the school curriculum and which are also generalizable to other areas.

Both current experimentation in schools and experimental studies of concept formation suggest that with superior teaching, children's understanding in a particular subject area or at least their ability to use vocabulary appropriately, can be considerably accelerated. Yet the net effect of such acceleration on intellectual development needs careful study. Some provocative work on Piaget concepts of conservation done by a Scandinavian psychologist, Smedslund (1961b), and a somewhat similar earlier investigation by Ausubel (1954) suggest that such acceleration sometimes results in what may be called pseudo-concepts. The child knows the answers only under conditions similar to those in which he learned them. Vary the conditions and he varies his answers. In contrast, the concepts acquired when the child is more mature tend to be stable and can be applied appropriately in many different situations.

It seems doubtful, therefore, that early childhood education programs that are narrowly focused or designed primarily for acceleration in a particular area will have much beneficial effect on later intellectual development. On the contrary, there is considerable reason to believe that each level of the hierarchy of intellectual development serves its own purposes and contributes uniquely to the next level.

One aspect of the early childhood period so far not considered here is imagination. The young child's lack of clear-cut, logically consistent categories for information may hamper his thinking in certain respects, but it also frees him to structure his world as he pleases. The color cone so carefully designed to teach him to deal with serial relationships can be a tree to embellish his block building, or a place to hang his cowboy hat, or a roll of telephone cable to carry in his truck. He can take it apart and use the pieces for food, or as parts of a necklace, or as spare tires. Just how such free ranging, playful thought relates itself to mature adult thinking is not very clear, though it is obvious that the highly intelligent adult who solves complex problems or arrives at new syntheses is by no

24

means limited to the logical thinking described by Piaget. He muses, wonders, glimpses analogies, gets caught up in fantasy in ways not very different from those revealed by the young child when he plays or paints or chants. Of course unlike the child, the adult can readily check the logic of the eventual outcome of his thought.

Perhaps metaphorical thought is too personal, too idiosyncratic to be nurtured in any particular way. Nevertheless, it is reassuring that current research in creativity and divergent thinking is beginning to move into the period of early childhood. Certainly no program intended to promote effective intellectual functioning in young children can overlook the importance of imagination in young children's thinking. Nor should it overlook the fact that the child's notion of play may differ from that of the adult. Indeed to plan only for the kind of play that the adult sees as a means to a particular end may be to stultify the initiative and interest that are essential to learning.

The point is illustrated by the four-year-old in an enrichment program in which the teacher, after noting that the child had successfully completed one puzzle, commented that he had learned that one well and inquired whether he would like to learn to do another one. The child, intent on his own purposes, replied, "No, but I'd like to *play* with it."

We come back thus to the cognitive child of our introduction. He is active, curious, interested; yet he is not completely manipulable. He has his own ways of thinking, his own ways of viewing the world. Whether or not he changes these ways depends only in part on what or whom he encounters. Change is equally dependent on what he thinks or feels he has to gain personally from his encounters.

New views on the nature of intellectual development open up new possibilities for influencing children's thinking, for guiding their encounters with the world in ways that will give them an increasingly better command over it. Such views need not, as some educators have feared, mean so exclusive a preoccupation with the intellect that other aspects of the child's being are necessarily neglected. Rather to the extent that teaching of this sort is based on understanding of the developing child and of his thinking and is able to free the child's intellect, it should also free him to be a more effective person.

References

1. D. Ausubel and S. Schiff. "The Effect of Incidental and Experimentally Induced Experience in the Learning of Relevant and Irrelevant Causal Relationships by Children." *Journal of Genetic Psychology* 84: 190-223; 1954.

2. J. S. Bruner. "The Viewpoint of a Psychologist." Review of B.

Inhelder and J. Piaget. *The Growth of Logical Thinking. British Journal of Psychology* 50: 363-70; 1959.

3. J. McV. Hunt. *Intelligence and Experience.* New York: Ronald Press, 1961.

4. B. Inhelder and J. Piaget. *The Growth of Logical Thinking from Childhood to Adolescence.* New York: Basic Books, 1958. (French edition 1955).

5. J. Piaget. *Judgment and Reasoning in the Child.* New York: Humanities Press, 1952. (1st French edition 1921).

6. J. Piaget. *The Language and Thought of the Child.* New York: Humanities Press, 1959. (1st French edition 1924).

7. J. Smedslund. "The Acquisition of Conservation of Substance and Weight in Children III. Extinction of Conservation of Weight Acquired 'Normally' and by Means of Empirical Controls on a Balance." *Scandinavian Journal of Psychology* 2: 85-87; 1961. (a).

8. J. Smedslund. "The Acquisition of Conservation of Substance and Weight in Children IV. Attempt at Extinction of the Visual Components of the Weight Concept." *Scandinavian Journal of Psychology* 2: 153-55; 1961. (b).

9. J. M. Tanner and B. Inhelder. *Discussions on Child Development.* Vol. 4. London: Tavistock Publications, 1960.

10. P. H. Wolff. "The Developmental Psychologies of Jean Piaget and Psychoanalysis." *Psychological Issues.* Volume 2, Number 1 (Monograph 5); 1960.

Cognitive Structures and Intellectual Processes

Donald M. Johnson

THIS paper will discuss cognitive structures, and the best place to begin is with concepts. We will start with the nature of concepts, and with tests for these, and pass on to other cognitive structures such as conceptual systems and principles. For purposes of this paper we need to know just what we mean by such abstract notions and what logic we use when we test for knowledge of each. Then we will consider the development of all these structures and their use in solving problems.[1]

The Nature of Concepts

An elementary way to structure the world is to construct or imagine a line, *e.g.*, a fence or a horizon, separating one part of the world from the rest. Another elementary way is to place similar objects together in groups so that similarities within groups and differences between groups can be readily perceived. Cognition or knowledge of an object then consists of the ability to place it in its proper group. A more sophisticated procedure is to assign certain objects to a general class, thus separating them conceptually from others. It is this type of cognitive structure, the class concept or general concept which is of most importance for education and which has been most studied by psychologists. Most of these classes are referred to by labels or names and most are also included in higher, supraordinate classes.

From the research standpoint a concept is not a fact that can be

[1] Thanks are due to Charlene O'Reilly for expert suggestions on a first draft of this paper.

observed, not a visible stimulus or response. Thus a concept is best treated as a hypothetical construct, like intelligence, that is intended to explain the observed facts. We do not observe intelligence, of course. We observe certain responses in certain standard situations, and on the basis of these observations and a background of previous study, we reason backward and infer that such responses required so much intelligence. Likewise, we observe a child putting balls, trains, guns and trucks in a box, and socks, shirts, sweaters and mittens in a drawer, so we infer that he has a concept of playthings and a concept of clothes. It would be hard to explain his behavior without making the inference that he knows playthings from clothes, yet it is an inference, nevertheless, and not a matter of direct observation.

A concept may be called a mediating construct since it is supposed to mediate between observable stimulus materials, *e.g.*, the socks, balls and shirts on one side, and observable responses, sorting them, on the other side. But since only the two ends are observed, we need a tight logical chain from observables to hypothetical construct to observables. If a student makes a test response presumed to demonstrate knowledge of the concept, we must ask if there is another way that he could make such a response before we give him credit for the concept. And if he fails, we must look for other parts of the chain where failure could occur before we conclude that the failure is due to lack of the concept.

Methods of Testing

Concepts are used in communication and in solving problems; yet when we want to test anyone's mastery of a particular concept, we usually arrange a testing situation with standard materials and standard instructions leading to responses that can be scored right or wrong. There are many kinds of tests for concepts because concept is a many-sided construct with a long history in education and psychology. These tests are sometimes grouped as multiple-choice tests and free-response tests, sometimes as performance tests and verbal tests. The performance tests may be called tests of skill while the verbal tests are called tests of knowledge. Experiments in the psychology laboratory, on which the discussion of concepts in most psychology books is founded, have typically been concerned with concepts based on a single common property, such as shape or color, or a systematic combination of a few such properties. Most standard concepts, however, such as sonnet, imperialism, and coelenterate, are based on several heterogeneous common properties, and these are the ones of most interest in research on intellectual development and educational achievement.

In any case, if we think of a concept as a class of objects, an appropriate multiple-choice test is to ask students to *classify* objects as members or nonmembers of the class. The instructions may be to sort coelenterates in one pile and other things in another pile, or to *label* the members of the class by one name and nonmembers by another name, or perhaps to underline pictures of members of the class. Success on such a test does not clearly prove that a concept has been mastered because it may be possible to associate specific objects with specific classes or labels. Hence a transfer test is often used, that is, the student is required to classify new objects that he has not had a chance to memorize. Failures also can be misinterpreted because the instructions may be misunderstood, especially by young children. They may be trying to memorize specific associations instead of discovering common properties. Some experiments have required the students to learn too many concepts at once, so that failure could be due not to inability to master any single concept but to interference in keeping the names straight. The reader is probably familiar with other multiple-choice tests, used for testing facts, that can also be used for testing concepts.

A common free-response method for demonstrating mastery of a concept can best be called *answers to questions*. Essay questions are widely used to sample achievement in an area of knowledge, but more specific questions directed toward a single standard concept of special importance have often been used in developmental studies. Short-answer questions are easier to evaluate, of course, and the classification task can be converted to short-answer questions: Given some examples, name the class. Given the class, name or draw some examples. Given some examples, name or draw others of the same class.

Description of a concept is a free-response test since it involves the production of drawings or words. The student may be asked to draw the common element in examples of figure concepts, to describe the common property of the class, to write a set of rules for classifying objects, or to define the word that labels a class.

The variability of output obtained by the free-response tests makes interpretation difficult. Memorizing must be considered as an alternative interpretation for success when definitions are requested because noncognitive association of a definition with a word is relatively easy. Likewise, interpretation of failure may be ambiguous because all free-response tests require some skill in drawing or writing and the deficiency may lie here rather than in the cognitive achievement itself.

In any case, when drawings and verbal answers are scored for research purposes, it is wise to have two or more judges evaluate each in respect to the relation between the production and the concept presumed to mediate the production. One new scoring scheme gives credit for common properties mentioned and subtracts for properties that are specific to single examples (Podell, 1958). When the scoring is carefully done, after some training for the judges, consistency between judges may be quite high. In one study three judges were used to rate the rules of classification written by students in a concept experiment, and the inter-judge correlations were about .80 (Shepard, Hovland and Jenkins, 1961).

It is obvious that any of these tests can be made in any degree of difficulty. Multiple-choice tests can require very subtle discrimination or gross discrimination between choices. Free-response tests can be scored strictly or generously.

Relation Between Tests of Concepts

When a concept is treated as a many-sided theoretical construct rather than a fact of observation, it is not surprising that there are several tests of it, as of intelligence and cost of living. The behavior used as an indicator of success or failure by each test is the joint result of the concept, which is theoretically independent of the test, and the instructions and test materials, which are peculiar to each test. Now the chief argument of this paper, the chief reason for this review of the tests is that the best evidence for achievement of a concept is success on two or more different tests of that concept. When we are trying to make inferences about a hypothetical construct, the logic of the case requires that two or more methods converge on this construct from different approaches (Garner, Hake and Eriksen, 1956). This seems to be a rather strict rule, and there may be many situations in which it can be ignored, yet when anyone is trying to prove that one way of teaching concepts is better than another or that it is necessary to master one concept before learning another, a critical methodology is necessary.

As a matter of fact, when two measures of concept achievement are used, they are likely to agree. In one experiment (Manis and Barnes, 1961) the subjects learn to classify airplane insignia as from friendly planes or from enemy planes and then answer the question: "How did you know which planes were friendly and which were enemy?" Those who could describe the concept to the experimenters' satisfaction were superior on the classification test to those who could not do so. Another experiment (Shepard, Hovland and Jenkins, 1961) had subjects classify complex collections of objects and also write rules for such classifications. Those problems that were difficult according to one measure were difficult according to the other. Such consistency is not surprising and has not aroused much discussion.

It is when two tests of concept achievement do not agree, or when the agreement is slight, that some explanation seems to be necessary.

For example, it has been demonstrated in psychology laboratories for forty years that some subjects can learn to classify objects correctly and then cannot state the basis of the classification. A Gallup Poll of a few years ago showed that ordinary citizens can classify public figures as radical, liberal, and conservative with considerable accuracy yet cannot give adequate definitions of these concepts. If we call the descriptions and definitions tests of knowledge, we can give these people credit for skilled performance without knowledge. The opposite discrepancy is illustrated by the complaint of teachers that some children can recall definitions of nouns and verbs but cannot identify these in sentences. There is a temptation to give these children credit for knowledge without the skill to do anything with it.

Actually this distinction between knowing and doing, or between knowledge and skill, is a fuzzy one that does not help us here in this abstract realm. In the light of the present argument it is better to consider these different tests as different ways of making inferences about the concept that presumably mediates the different response measures. If the student passes two or more tests of the same concept, he has mastered the concept. If he fails all of them, he has not mastered the concept. If he passes one and fails another, we have to admit that the results are ambiguous. We can go further and point out reasons for the inconsistencies because they are important for the design of studies of concept learning and perhaps for methods of teaching concepts.

One obvious reason for a discrepancy is that, whether the concept itself is easy or hard, one test of it may be harder than another. One test may have clearer instructions than another. Or the response measure may be easier than another. Multiple-choice measures, for example, are easier than free-response measures; hence classification tests are easier than writing definitions. One way to reduce this discrepancy would be to write two definitions and require the student to choose the better of the two, just as he chooses the better of two labels for an object. This would equate the two types of test in form and go one step toward equating them in difficulty.

Another reason for a discrepancy is that one response has usually been practiced or studied more than the other. In many concept-learning experiments the classification response is practiced from the beginning, then later the subject is asked to compose a definition or to describe the common property, tasks which he has not previously practiced. Or, in reverse, students may acquire considerable book knowledge about classes of microorganisms before they have a chance to look into a microscope and actually try to classify the specimens they see. It follows that if practice on different types of tests is equated, the discrepancies in the results will be reduced.

Other Cognitive Structures

A class concept may be considered a simple cognitive structure of two regions, inside and outside. We should also mention conceptual dimensions or qualities that vary along a scale, such as temperature, intelligence and virtue. A large part of education consists of the acquisition of systems of concepts of all kinds, and these of course are cognitive structures of higher levels of abstractness and complexity. A few familiar examples are: taxonomic systems for classifying plants and animals, relations between governmental agencies at local, state, national and international levels, and the interrelated concepts of modern chemistry.

Most important of all are principles, generalizations or laws, which are relations between concepts. Visual acuity increases as illumination increases. Aggression arises out of frustration. $S = \frac{1}{2}gt^2$. Put many of these concepts and relations together, as in mathematics and science, and you have an abstract cognitive structure far removed from observable facts but logically related to observable facts and necessary for understanding of the facts. It is these conceptual structures, that psychologists neglected for many years and that some educators said children could not learn, that are now the focus of renewed attention, as in Chapter 2 of Bruner's book, *The Process of Education* (1960).

Mastery of these structures or segments of them is tested by the variety of tests used for concepts, frequently by the test of application or transfer to new situations. That is, in addition to statement of a principle and classification of situations to which it applies, we can ask the student to use it to solve a problem. The different tests of mastery of these more complex cognitive structures do not always agree, for the same reasons that different tests of single concepts do not always agree. Some students can state a principle but cannot apply it, and vice versa. The best evidence is success on two or more different tests.

Development and Use of Cognitive Structures

The observable responses associated with cognitive structures are learned, like other things, in several ways. The young child learns in an elementary way, perhaps by operant conditioning, to put things to play with in one place and things to wear in another place, and so on. He learns casually in daily communication to make appropriate responses to words used by adults, perhaps by classical conditioning and stimulus generalization. There is a question, as I have said, whether a concept is demonstrated by either kind of response alone, but when the child does the classifying and also uses the conventional words to describe the class, we are quite sure he has the concept, and this kind of learning is not so casual. At least we know that it goes better by active problem solving, as when the child deliberately tries to pinpoint the distinction between one class of objects and another and when he puzzles over the meaning of a new word. Of course the child learns even better when someone helps him by identifying common properties, by confirming good guesses, by arranging materials so that similarities and differences are readily perceived.

The same statements can be made for the learning of principles. Consider the principle that the angle of incidence equals the angle of reflection. One way to approach it is to memorize this nine-word sentence. Another way is to practice catching a ball bounced off a wall. Progress can be made by either of these approaches, but neither contributes much to mastery of the principle. It takes a higher form of learning, an active search for the stated principle in the incidence and reflection of the ball, usually with the help of a teacher or textbook. After the principle is discovered in the observed facts, it is more readily applied to new situations, as when light bounces off a mirror or a billiard ball bounces off the cushion at right angles.

We all know the chief difficulties in learning concepts and principles. By definition these things are abstract, and the more abstract they are, the harder they are to learn. Much of the information in courses on methods and materials of teaching consists of techniques for making the abstract more concrete, for making the common properties more apparent. And, in reverse, the task of identifying a common feature in a number of examples is made more difficult by the pattern in which the common feature is embedded. Many children classify whales among the fishes because their similarities to fish are obvious while their similarities to other mammals are hidden. Living in the water is irrelevant information as far as classification of a mammal is concerned, and experiments have shown that difficulty of concept achievement increases directly with the number of such irrelevant details (Archer, Bourne and Brown, 1955). Here again, teachers, textbooks and audiovisual aids make concept learning easier by emphasizing or isolating the essential feature of several examples so that it will stand out from the surrounding entanglements. All this, I believe, is standard doctrine.

When we ask what is the best way to program such learning, what is the optimal sequence for presenting the material, the answers are not so standard, and teachers have to work these out specifically for their own materials and their own students. One of the gains to be expected from the recent increase of interest in programed learning is that different sequences will probably be tried out and their results compared.

What I would suggest for trial, aside from the standard suggestions, is a policy of alternation: alternation between the specific and the general, between performance tests and verbal tests, between the multiple-choice format and the free-response format. Just as the best evidence for mastery of a concept consists of two or more tests, the best program for learning concepts and principles would consist of two or more types of practice. One type might be the performance type, working problems and applying principles, and another might be a more verbal type, discussion of such concepts and principles. According to the present point of view, alternation between these types of study would be better than the same amount of time spent on either one alone. I am not familiar with any research bearing directly on this point, but it should be easy to test this out. Classifying nouns and verbs in sentences should make it easier to define these and describe their functions. Defining and describing should make classification easier. Going back and forth between the two types of study should promote deeper and broader understanding and transfer to new examples. This would have to be true, I believe, if the final criterion of mastery of these concepts includes two or more kinds of tests.

We want students, at all grade levels, to learn the big generalizations and principles, the abstract cognitive structures, because they can be applied to new situations in higher grades and outside of school. They transfer better than the specific examples on which they are based. From what I read, educational theory and curriculum planning, after worshipping at the door of specifics for many years, may now be turning again to the big generalizations and introducing these at lower grades. I expect to hear any day that psychoanalysis is being programed for the second grade (this suggestion, however, is more likely to come from a consultant than from a teacher). I suggest that if the teacher tries out three programs, one dealing largely with specific facts, one dealing largely with general principles, and one that goes back and forth between the specific and the general, the last will be the most efficient. This is an obvious principle, but it requires firsthand knowledge of students and subject matter to introduce specifics and generalities at the proper level of difficulty. The best sequence would presumably start with specific components at the right level of difficulty and move as rapidly as possible to general principles of a higher level of abstraction, then back to more specifics, then on to generalizations of a still higher level, and so on. These variations have to be tested out for each subject matter at each grade because one could err by too much drill on specifics or by too rapid a jump to the high-level principles.

Another caution that should be mentioned, though I am sure it is familiar to many teachers, is that solving a problem once does not mean thorough mastery (Adams, 1954). It is better to solve several before going on to a broader range of problems, probably because one can get a right answer once or twice without thorough knowledge of the principle. After several problems of one type have been worked, transfer to problems of a different type is easier.

The structure of knowledge changes and our society changes. Although the facts may not change much, the explanatory concepts and principles that seemed important when we went to school may not be the important ones for our students today. New conceptual systems that are hard for the teacher to master may actually be easier for the student who begins by learning the facts in the new framework. Apparently the mathematics of sets is not so difficult when introduced early as it is to us who have to learn it late. I would venture the guess that there are worthwhile generalizations in history and geography, not ordinarily studied until graduate school, that could be learned in the elementary grades. Certainly there are many concepts and principles of modern scientific psychology, usually introduced in college, that could be mastered much earlier if properly programed. This is just another way of saying that it is the responsibility of teachers and textbook writers to keep up to date in the big abstractions as well as the little details. Since I struggled with this problem recently in writing a textbook of psychology for college students, I cannot do better than quote a paragraph from the preface.

As psychological research increases in amount and depth, it is possible to correct the omissions and errors of the past by adding more information on each topic. The better approach, of course, is not addition but selection and reorganization. Instead of teaching the student Binet's conception of the IQ and the modern additions, it is better to teach him the modern conception at the outset. It is better to skip the ancient concept of fatigue and its inadequacies and start the student out with a modern concept of work that need not be immediately updated. Conceptual reorganizations achieved at advanced levels, as well as new facts, should be moved down to the elementary level as soon as possible (Johnson, 1961a).

Cognitive Structures and Problem Solving

Now let us turn to the work we have been doing at Michigan State and describe briefly some experiments on problem solving. The first one is a thesis (Bremer, 1962) which shows how cognitive structures can help and hinder the solution of problems. The problems were anagram problems, done in college classes in the usual way, but different groups had different kinds of previous experience with the words which were the solutions to the anagrams. Immediately before working the anagrams one group was given each word in isolation and asked to rate it for pleasantness. Another group had these words in short phrases and another in sentences to rate for pleasantness. As expected, all of these groups solved more anagrams than a control group without any previous experience with these words. Yet those who had the words in isolation did best on the anagrams. Those who had the words in phrases were next, and those with the sentences profited least by this experience. Why? Because when the words were read in sentences, they were embedded in larger cognitive structures and therefore not retained in a form that could later be utilized for problem solving. In another experiment we had the words of the anagrams exposed to the subjects while they were struggling with the anagrams, but they did not use the hints in front of their eyes. Why? Because the words were buried in the instructions for the experiment, printed at the top of the answer sheet. In these cases it is not the structure that was difficult to understand. Quite the reverse. The structure of a sentence, or a phrase, was so well understood as a whole that the single words were not well perceived and retained.

Several of our experiments have attempted to describe problem solving activities or cognitive processes. If facts, memories, concepts and other cognitive structures are the raw materials of thought, cognitive processes are the operations performed on them. The differentiation of the problem-solving enterprise into a few thought processes is an ancient aspiration, and most readers are probably familiar with John Dewey's (1910) analysis of "how we think" into five steps. We find it most convenient to speak of three thought processes: preparation, production and judgment (Johnson, 1955).

Since preparation goes quickly and is probably the location of many errors, we tried to identify this operation by a serial-exposure apparatus which permits the subject to do what he wants to do but also permits us to follow each operation and time it (Johnson, 1961b). Ten geometrical figures are shown on the left side of the exposure apparatus and the subject is instructed to observe what they have in common, then to turn a switch illuminating a display of figures on the right side and find another example of the same class. The first operation, which is preparatory to the second, would be called formulation in this particular problem. The thinker formulates the problem by studying the ten figures to identify the common property or concept, then he tries to find another figure at the right that also possesses this property. In our ambiguous test problems there were only two common properties, shape and texture, and two corresponding solutions. The subject who formulates a problem in terms of shape will pick one solution, and the subject who formulates it in terms of texture will pick a different one. This formulation, of course, is another kind of cognitive structure.

Our first hypothesis was that those subjects who work a series of problems with easy shape solutions will formulate them in terms of shape and get set to look for shape similarities, so when they meet an ambiguous problem, they will choose the shape solution. Likewise, those who work a series of problems with easy texture solutions will choose a texture solution for the same ambiguous problem. We ran two groups with such contrasted pretraining and found that a high percentage of the solutions to the ambiguous test problems agreed with this hypothesis. Hence we can infer this hypothetical cognitive structure, the formulation, from observable data, and we have an additional check on the inference because we can slant the formulation one way or the other by a few preliminary problems.

Now if the thinker's formulation is inadequate and he cannot find a solution to match it, he will have to reformulate the problem and search for another type of solution. To study this, we introduced a modification in the procedure, telling the subjects that they could switch back and examine the ten figures on the left again if necessary, and such switchbacks, something like regressive eye movements in reading, were taken as objective indicators of reformulation. We ran a group of subjects with practice on easy shape problems and then gave them an ambiguous problem without a shape solution. Our prediction was that they would formulate it in terms of shape and look for a shape solution, but, since they would not find one, they would switch back, reformulate it in terms of texture, return and look for a texture solution, and thus solve the problem on the second try. Those with practice on texture problems were given the reverse problems, with the reverse prediction. The results came out as expected. Each subject switched back at the proper time, and then solved the problem the other way. Thus we claim that we have identified and timed four intellectual operations in sequence: (a) the first formulation of the problem, (b) the unsuccessful search for a solution to match this formulation, (c) switchback and reformulation, and (d) successful search for a solution to match the second formulation.

In another study of cognitive processes in problem solving we investigated the judgment of the solutions produced as well as their production (Johnson and Zerbolio). We had college students produce titles for short plots because previous research has shown that this is a good test of originality and because it is feasible for students to write plot titles and to judge them critically. There were two questions: Will practice in judgment improve production? Will practice in production improve judgment? So we had college students read short plots with a number of suggested titles for each and to practice judging the cleverness of the titles on a scale of 1 to 5, checking each judgment against the judgment of experts. Then they read other plots and wrote titles for these. As compared to control groups who merely read titles, there was no superiority of production due to the practice in judging. Another group wrote titles for practice and then judged a standard series of titles which had been judged by experts. This practice in production was definitely effective in improving the accuracy of judgment. Another group with direct practice in judgment did not improve in judgment.

These results are not peculiar to plot titles. Another thesis (Howat, 1962) used a perceptual-motor task which permitted judgment of how far a pendulum would travel and also production of a required amount of travel. Quite similar results were obtained. Practice in production improved judgment more than did practice in judgment.

How can this be? We have all learned that the best way to master something is to work at it. Yet these experiments demonstrate that the best way to improve judgment is not to practice judgment but to practice production. Our interpretation is that in order to make good judgments one has to learn the dimension or quality to be judged. In this case one has to learn the dimension of cleverness of plot titles, which is another kind of cognitive structure or concept. And it is possible to make judgments on a scale of cleverness by assigning numbers to titles without really understanding this dimension of cleverness. But if one is forced to write some clever plot titles, he has to come to grips with the meaning of cleverness and thus can better tell a clever title when he sees one. This seems to back up the statement we hear from college students that the best way to study for a multiple-choice examination is not to study for a multiple-choice examination but to study for an essay examination. In the process of organizing one's ideas and getting ready to write something one learns the conceptual relations or structure of the material more thoroughly than if one merely gets ready to make choices.

Now if we can stretch the significance of these experiments a little further, we would say that they support the custom of appointing book reviewers and editors who have had some experience in writing as well as the practice of having students write something as preparation for evaluating the writings of others. They do not support the hope that reading and evaluating the writings of others will improve their own writing.

References

J. A. Adams. "Multiple Versus Single Problem Training in Human Problem Solving." *Journal of Experimental Psychology* 48: 15-18; 1954.

E. J. Archer, L. E. Bourne and F. G. Brown. "Concept Identification as a Function of Irrelevant Information and Instructions." *Journal of Experimental Psychology* 49: 153-64; 1955.

Bradley A. Bremer. Unpublished M.A. Thesis. East Lansing: Michigan State University, 1962.

J. S. Bruner. *The Process of Education.* Cambridge: Harvard University Press, 1960.

J. Dewey. *How We Think.* Boston: D. C. Heath and Company, 1910.

W. R. Garner, H. W. Hake and C. W. Eriksen. "Operationism and the Concept of Perception." *Psychological Review* 63: 149-59; 1956.

M. G. Howat. Unpublished Ph.D. Dissertation. East Lansing: Michigan State University, 1962.

D. M. Johnson. *The Psychology of Thought and Judgment.* New York: Harper & Brothers, 1955.

D. M. Johnson. "Formulation and Reformulation of Figure-Concepts." *American Journal of Psychology* 74: 418-24; 1961b.

D. M. Johnson. *Psychology: A Problem Solving Approach.* New York: Harper & Brothers, 1961a.

D. M. Johnson and D. J. Zerbolio. "Relations Between Production and Judgment of Plot Titles." *American Journal of Psychology.* In press.

M. Manis and E. J. Barnes. "Learning Without Awareness and Mediated Generalization." *American Journal of Psychology* 74: 425-32; 1961.

H. A. Podell. "Two Processes of Concept Formation." *Psychological Monographs.* Volume 72, Number 468; 1958.

R. N. Shepard, C. I. Hovland and H. M. Jenkins. "Learning and Memorization of Classifications." *Psychological Monographs.* Volume 75, Number 517; 1961.

Curiosity and Exploration: Roles in Intellectual Development and Learning

SINCE man first developed self-awareness, he has attempted to discover those things that cause him to behave as he does. The road to discovery has been tortuous. Man is such a complex organism and the means by which to assess his behavior are so inadequate that progress has proceeded at a snail-like pace. Yet what has caused even more difficulty is our eagerness and our predetermined notions about the nature of man. Eagerness and predetermination cause one to overlook facts and arrive at erroneous formulations. They also cause the researcher to channel his investigations along certain lines while ignoring other lines of investigation.

Educators as a group have been no different from other people in their attempts to explain how school children behave and learn. The great sin and danger in the explanation of any type of human behavior is that of oversimplifying that which we are attempting to explain. This tendency to oversimplify leads us to assume that learning in one curriculum area is the same as learning in another curriculum area, that problem solving in a testing situation is the same as problem solving in a non-testing situation and that school learning is the same as non-school learning.

By the same mode of thinking we assume that, because there is an intellect, it is immediately useable to the person. Such an assumption makes it easy for us to administer standardized tests of achievement, arrive at a grade expectancy score and then expect that a child be achiev-

40

ing at a level commensurate with the score. The dictum of this assumption is that there are no variables that intervene between the intellect and the manifestation of the intellect.

While on the one hand we conceive of the intellect as not being affected by other human factors, we speak on the other hand of "motivation." Admittedly, our statements about motivation are rather vague, but almost intuitively we recognize that there are factors that affect the manifestation of the intellect. Perhaps it is what we see when we look around us in the school setting that predisposes us to give credence to "non-intellectual" factors that influence learning. We observe cases of children with low intellectual ability but who have an avidity for experience and who progress well, even if not with distinction, in school. More likely is it that we note cases in which there is high intellectual ability but in which performance is low. We refer to the possible causation of the behavior of these two types of children as being one of "motivation."

Both psychologists and educators historically have not made distinction as to certain types of motives, but rather have treated the term in a global manner. Only in a peripheral and nontechnical sense has there been any differentiation. For example, it is not too unusual to hear teachers refer to given children as "curious," "inquisitive" or "exploratory." Clearly, there were some behaviors which led to the teachers' comments, but we are not certain what the precise behaviors were, nor whether the behaviors were caused by a motive or some personality factor. The term used with great frequency by teachers is that of "curiosity." It is the central purpose of this paper to discuss this variable that apparently intervenes between the intellect and its manifestation. While the major focus will be on curiosity as a factor that influences the intellect and learning, we will also take a brief excursion into the area of exploratory behavior.

A Basis for Epistemic Behavior

By epistemic behavior we mean any behavior that augments knowledge; a drive that is reducible by input of information from the environment to the individual. Viewed in this way it is apparent that epistemic behavior can be used somewhat synonymously with curiosity. It is also apparent that curiosity has to do with the way in which a person deals with or interacts with his environment.

In the process of growing up and experiencing, a child has many contacts with varied aspects of his environment. These "contacts" become incorporated into his cognitive structure. This cognitive structure is much like a private map that the individual has of his world. In it there are objects, persons and institutions, each of which is accorded color, temperature, odor, weight and shape, to name a few qualities. What is even more important is that each of these aspects of the cognitive map has valence to the individual. That is to say, some aspects have positive valuation while others have negative. Those having positive valence are "closer" to the individual in his cognitive structure, while those with negative valence are more distant. Conceivably, the more positive aspects are those toward which the individual is able to direct his behavior and the more negative aspects cause the child to engage in avoidance behavior.

The organism depends on stimuli for the information which goes into the cognitive map. The stimuli are used as information about the environment and then one's motor behavior is guided by the information. What is learned is more than information and is more than simply motor behavior; the learning has been perceptual-motor. In other words, we must give credit to the organism as having more than effectors and receptors. Of paramount importance is that the learner has the capacities for using stimuli to produce results within himself and within his external environment.

A child uses his cognitive map to make predictions from the past to the present situation. In so doing he assumes that the present environment is identical to or highly similar to what it was in the past. Ordinarily this is a good assumption and benefits the child since his expectancies permit him to organize in such a way as to make optimal use of both time and resources. What must be emphasized is that the individual is actually making hypotheses about the stimuli that he will be receiving. What happens if the anticipated stimuli are not encountered? Sometimes the environment has changed in relatively important ways and hypotheses are not fulfilled (29).

It is entirely probable that the organism does not expect or anticipate that the present situation will be identical with those of the past. The young child may make such predictions from his cognitive structure, but with increased experience it would be anticipated that there would be change. Thus, the anticipation of change is partially an *experiential matter*. The role of change in stimuli will be discussed in a different context later. The child faces the present situation then with two anticipations: (a) the environment will be, in the main, comparable with what it was in the past, and (b) there will be change in the environment. As experience accumulates, it is probable that the child savors the novelty of change in the environment and that this becomes the basis for epistemic (curiosity) behavior. These novel stimuli lead the individual to a response which, in turn, leads to a drive stimulus which we shall call curiosity. Curiosity then predisposes a person to engage in exploratory behavior. However, continued exposure to the novel, curiosity-producing stimuli causes curiosity to decrease (10).

The last point made is one that needs emphasis. Originally all stimuli possess properties of novelty and the only difference between the novel and the unnovel stimuli is that the former have not lost their original effects. This is readily observable in the behavior of young children who are presented an object or toy which occupies them for a period of time. However, it is not long before they drop the object and cast about for something of new interest. The object has lost its novelty; examination and exploration cease because there has been stimulus satiation. The typical teacher refers to this in terms of the child's "attention span."

The novel stimulus is like all other novel stimuli in the sense that it has the same potential capacity for inducing conflict in the individual. The role of conflict in epistemic behavior is central. For example, when the novel stimulus is encountered it evokes in the person a host of possible responses. Some of these possible responses are incompatible, therefore causing conflict and arousing curiosity. Greater uncertainty or conflict is caused the more nearly the possible responses reach equaprobability, *i.e.*, the more nearly each is similar to all others as being the proper response to be made in the given situation.

It will be noted that our description thus far has been rather situationally oriented in the respect that the external environment has been emphasized. Two factors have not been discussed that may have some role in the curiosity behavior of man. One of these is personality structure. It has been implied that the cognitive map a person has is an aspect of personality and that it influences perception of stimuli. In a later section of this paper, the role of personality correlates is discussed more fully. But we hasten to affirm the fact that curiosity is evoked by stimuli which provide the organism with data or information. These data are "processed" by the organism—and we hypothesize that the self is the data processor of the organism.

Another factor which has not been discussed is the role that neurology might play in the matter of change in stimulation. There is no direct answer to the question of whether the nervous system *requires* stimulation. On the other hand, we do have information from the studies on perceptual isolation and sensory deprivation that suggests affirmative answers. Bexton, Heron and Scott (26) report deficient problem solving plus visual hallucination in male college students following a period of reduced sensory input. Each volunteer stayed isolated in a semi-sound-proof cubicle for 2 to 3 days, fitted with goggles which admitted patternless, diffuse light, wearing gloves and cuffs limiting tactual stimuli, and hearing only a vague hum from an air conditioner. The subjects were tested both within the cubicle (oral problem solving and associative learning tests) and by standard tests after release from the cubicle. The experimental group test results immediately after isolation were inferior to a control group on 6 of 7 tests. Testing during isolation showed an inferior performance on all tests for the experimental group, with significant differences on anagrams, word-making and requests for repetition. Subjective reports from the subjects described difficulty in concentrating, blank periods, confusion and visual hallucination progressing from simple dots or lines to complex scenes over which the subjects reported little control.

In another experiment (26), researchers tested perception and recorded electroencephalograph readings on 12 experimental subjects and 20 controls, under the above-mentioned conditions. Perceptual tests were administered the day before the 96-hour isolation period. EEG records were taken twice daily during isolation, during hallucinatory periods, and at the end of and following isolation. Visual disturbances were reported by the subjects upon removing their goggles. For some, these disturbances lasted several hours, were classified as movement of objects; warping of surfaces; curving of horizontal lines; displacement of parallel lines; movement of objects accompanying movement of subject; strong after-images; and increases in color, contrast and shine. The experimental subjects tested less accurately on tactual and spatial perception tasks. The EEG records indicated progressively lower brain activity during isolation, persisting for some subjects three or more hours after release. The subjects in this test slept a good deal at the beginning of the experiment and then became progressively more wakeful.

One can make a distinction between sensory deprivation and perceptual isolation. In the former the environment is set up in such a way that the subjects' receptors are prevented from being stimulated; in perceptual isolation, patterned stimuli are eliminated without reducing intensity of physical energy impinging upon the receptors. One may theorize that as a result of either of these deprivations receptor activity is reduced and the threshold of sensory neurones is lowered, resulting in change of or failure of neural organization. Whatever the case, it is apparent that stimuli are needed in constant supply, they must have relevance and must be variant from previous stimuli.

There is a story about a man who was asked a difficult question. He responded to his inquisitor by saying, "I understand your words, sir. It is the sentences that cause me trouble." Yet what if we do not even understand the words? This is an oblique way of getting to the point that we use the word "curiosity" in our everyday language and really do not understand the specifics of its meaning.

We ask a question of a person and he, in turn, asks why the question was posed. We often answer by saying, "I was just curious." Or we say to a colleague, "I am curious to know why so and so did that." Teachers refer to various pupils as being curious or not curious. In each of the examples there is some connotation of probing into something, of attempting to extend one's knowledge.

A person may be said to manifest curiosity when his behavior is such as to cause him to: scan his environment seeking new experiences; respond positively to new, ambiguous or incongruous aspects of the environment by approaching, investigating and manipulating these; increase verbal activity that evokes information from other people; avoid the more familiar aspects of the environment; be persistent in examining stimuli after contact has been made with them (7, 16).

From the preceding, it becomes apparent that curiosity leads to increase in the quantity of sensory data input since the curious person is attending to a larger environment. The curious organism is "tuned," it does not see but it *looks for*, it does not hear but it does *listen for*. Being so "tuned," curiosity increases the clarity of the objects that are perceived. One might say the objects are more differentiated in the perceptual field. More important to the educator, perhaps, is the fact that curiosity has the potential for furthering the cognitive schema of a person. The child's cognitive map is broadened. This must inevitably alter the symbolic repertoire of the curious child. Hopefully the alteration of the symbol system is such that learning is facilitated. Viewed in these ways it can be said that curiosity is one human dynamic that makes the intellect operational.

Studies of Curiosity in Laboratory Settings

The experimental study of curiosity is in its relative infancy. Until fairly recently there was no research on the subject that had as its major intent the discovery or description of some aspect of curiosity. Said in a different way, there was earlier research but the investigator was not primarily interested in curiosity or epistemic behavior. Therefore, his research findings were used to infer what curiosity was or the role it played in human development. Some of the earlier studies used animals as subjects. Berlyne (2) studied the epistemic behavior of rats by confronting them with an unfamiliar space in the maze. Later he added a variety of new objects to the unfamiliar space. With the addition of each new object the rats were found to approach, sniff and examine. However, these behaviors subsided rather quickly until a new object was added which restored nearly to original strength the sniffing and examining behavior. Much the same type of behavior was observed by Welker (27) who confronted chimpanzees with pairs of objects and noted the interest elicited. The chimps would at first approach the objects in a cautious manner, then would examine at length, handle fully and then discard the object. When Welker introduced a new pair of objects, the sequence was repeated. The similarity of both the rats' behavior and the chimps' behavior should be noted. Each regarded with caution, examined lightly, discovered fully, discarded and then repeated the foregoing when new objects were presented to them.

Educators, as a group, have violence done to their finer sensibilities when research involving subhumans is related to them. They are to be commended for this stand since behavior of a less complex organism can be somewhat different, to say the very least, from the behavior of a more complex organism. Suffice it to say, then, that while the large area of study of curiosity is a Johnny-come-lately on the research scene, the study of curiosity in humans is an even more recent activity. Even though new, the information is germane to this discourse.

In earlier studies the introduction of novelty to elicit curiosity was sometimes referred to in the context of subjects' attention to change (3). A case in point is the study in which service personnel were presented with one or more of four visual stimuli whose color and shape could be varied. Each stimulus had its own Morse key which was to be pressed in response to it. When a combination of one or more stimuli appeared, the subjects were told to respond to one only, the choice being left to their discretion. Response to the chosen stimulus was considered an objective manifestation of the person's attention to that stimulus. Both shape and color of the stimuli were changed in a given sequence. It was found that in all phases of the experiment there was a significant tendency for subjects to respond to the changed stimulus rather than the unchanged. This tendency was especially apparent when the stimulus changed progressively and periodically. It was concluded that a recently changed stimulus has greater chance of being responded to than one that has remained unchanged (has been responded to). It was concluded also, that when only one stimulus remained unchanged and several other stimuli changed, the effect mentioned was not so apparent.

We must raise questions at this point as to what these results might mean to a teacher. If the stimuli in a classroom remain unchanged, *e.g.*, relatively long periods of "seat work," is it conceivable that a new stimulus, such as a sneeze, titter or shuffling of feet, diverts attention from the educative work and directs attention to the new stimulus? Conversely, does the teacher do himself and the students a disservice when he introduces new stimuli into the teaching-learning situation at such a rate that they take precedence in number over unchanged or previously attended-to stimuli? To be more accurate, we raise once again the issue of the *pacing* of introduction of stimuli into the learning situation as well as their newness. This we have referred to previously as the "flow concept."

Curiosity and the newness or novelty of stimuli have received attention through research activity. The first few paragraphs of this section describe experiments in which animals manifested certain behaviors upon being presented new objects. It is interesting to reflect on those studies in relation to attempts to discover how humans respond to complexity and novelty in their environment. Sixteen undergraduates were the subjects for an investigation in which an attempt was made to ascertain the relation between conflict and curiosity (5). Each subject took part in four phases of the experiment consisting of a key-pressing response when presented with visual figures projected by means of a tachistoscope. The students were free to have as many exposures of each figure as they wished. Certain properties of the figures were found to increase curiosity significantly: incongruity (when out of a series of seven pictures of birds two were incongruous); and surprisingness (of 12 cards having geometric patterns, the first six had red triangles, the next five had green circles and the twelfth had a violet square).

It could be disputed that in the foregoing experiment key pressing did not give an indication of curiosity arousal because the subject observed one figure at a time and could conjure up some dimension of novelty even if there were none. In other words, there was no competition between stimuli. A different experiment by the same person (6) tested the degree to which changing features in stimuli attracted more visual fixation than recurrent features. Twenty college undergraduates were shown two figures simultaneously. One member of each pair of slides was less complex and the other more complex. Complexity was represented by different categories: (a) irregularity of arrangement of the figures; (b) amount of material in the figures; (c) heterogeneity of elements, in which spatial arrangement was the same but the elements of the figure different; (d) irregularity of shape; and (e) incongruity of figures (normal bird and an incongruous bird). The experimenter was to determine which of the two figures the subject fixated on first and how long he fixated. The results showed that for every pair there was greater fixation time on the more complex figure and that this result was significant beyond the .01 level for each of the five categories.

So far the findings of these studies of curiosity have been consistent, namely, that there is a preference for stimuli which are more complex and more non-homeostatic. The consistency of these findings is broken only by a very recent (7) study, in which the subjects were asked to make a choice between a more irregular design and less irregular design. This was done by presenting each of the two designs of a pair in succession and then asking the S (subject) which one he would like to see again. He could see either design again by taking a card from a tray which was appropriately marked. There were 18 pairs of designs in all.

The results indicate that there was a tendency for these undergraduate students to make preponderantly LI (less irregular) choices or preponderantly MI (more irregular) choices. This bimodal tendency is in contrast to the other studies in which there was a modal tendency. One possible explanation is that factors other than those in the environment were in play, *i.e.*, more personological factors influenced the results. While this is pure speculation, it should be noted that personality variables have not been considered in the researches cited.

Studies of Curiosity in Educational Settings

There is a considerable body of theoretical formulations and experimental research using animal subjects. One is always tempted to generalize the findings from animal subjects to human subjects. To do so represents the nadir of thinking, for this would then lead us to making generalizations about what a curriculum might be like for the human subjects. This would place us in the unenviable position of making curricular decisions for human beings on the basis of research findings using subhumans as subjects. Fortunately, educators have not only resisted such temptations in the past, but they have been adamant in their resistance.

It is worth repeating that the study of curiosity is in its relative infancy, but we are reassured by the fact that some of the investigations of curiosity behavior have been done with school-aged children in school situations. Typical of these is a study by Mittman and Terrell (19). These investigators sought to determine the effects of three levels of curiosity on the selection by first and second grade children of size and form discrimination problems. Each of 42 subjects was required to learn the size and form of a given object. With each trial he could then connect two successive dots on a dot drawing (either an elephant standing on its hind legs, or a dog begging). The subjects were randomly divided into three groups representing levels of curiosity: high curiosity, moderate curiosity, and low curiosity. For the low curiosity group the experimenter presented the completed dot drawing immediately following the instructions and just prior to the first trial in size and form discrimination. The completed drawing was shown to subjects of the moderate and high curiosity groups after the 8th and 29th correct responses, respectively, to the size and form discrimination problems. There was a significant difference in the number of errors committed by subjects of the high, moderate and low curiosity groups. The rank order of the three groups in terms of number of errors committed was low, moderate and high.

What is particularly noteworthy about the study cited above is that the subjects were not selected on the basis of some measures of curiosity.

Instead, the environment was structured in such a way as to create uncertainty or curiosity in the children. This would suggest that the researcher may create curiosity by the instructional procedures that he uses. The study suggests also that high curiosity enables a person to gain greater precision in his learning (fewer errors in size and form discrimination).

As we shall see, many investigations of curiosity, novelty or uncertainty focus on the degree to which ambiguity is tolerable to the individual. This is reflected in the research done to determine the relation between qualitatively different types of environmental novelty and curiosity in children (24). The subjects were 44 first grade children, half of whom were boys. Each of the subjects was seated before a mock TV set in which two filmstrips were placed. The strips contained sets of stimuli presented in different order for a variety of tasks. The mock TV set contained a response panel on which there were a button and a lever. Each time the subject pressed the button a picture was repeated on the TV screen for 250 milliseconds. Pulling the lever permitted the subject to change to a new picture. The subjects were tested on three tasks, stimulus ambiguity (SA), in which one set of stimuli was patterned and the other random; perceptual conflict (PC), in which two sets of pictures of animals and birds were presented that were congruous or incongruous with their previous perceptions; and, conceptual conflict (CC), in which six pictures were utilized which began with a circle and by progressive addition of details ended with a complete picture.

When the data were analyzed it was found that novel (incongruous, random) stimuli elicited significantly more responses than non-novel pictures (P .001). One could say on the basis of this finding that novelty generally evoked positive approach behavior. There was also a significant difference between the boys' and girls' performance. The girls were curious when confronted with an environment lacking in information necessary to complete a spatial or temporal pattern of events, but were relatively lacking in response when incongruous objects were presented to them. In short, the girls were found to be more rigid and less curious than the boys. Apparently, rigidity and curiosity are negatively associated.

In the studies previously cited, it was assumed that to a certain degree all of the subjects possessed curiosity and an attempt was made to ascertain the impact of a modified environment upon curiosity. The studies to be discussed take a somewhat different theoretical position in the respect that groups of children are identified as having different degrees of curiosity motivation and their performance on certain types of tasks is assessed.

Earlier the statement was made that educators appear to believe that there are no factors intervening between the intellect and learning.

A recent experiment (12a) gives evidence that allows us to examine the belief. The experimenters hypothesized that children with high curiosity amass a larger store of general information than do children of the same intelligence who have low curiosity. The hypothesis was tested by selecting groups of fifth grade children of high and low curiosity and comparing their scores on a test of general information. The curiosity groups were established on the basis of teacher and peer judgments of curiosity. Intelligence was statistically controlled. The groups were similar in age, popularity and tested intelligence. A test of general information, consisting of items based on material in encyclopedias available to children, discriminated in favor of the high curiosity children.

A skeptic might raise the question as to whether children with high curiosity retain their knowledge after it has once been learned. Maw and Maw (13) addressed themselves to such a question in another study using approximately 800 fifth grade children as subjects. In this study it was hypothesized that retention is due, at least in part, to the level of curiosity children have about their environment. Children high and low in curiosity were identified, using teacher and peer judgments. The children were given copies of a story which was a collection of strange but true facts, mostly about animal subjects. As far as the children were concerned the experience ended with the experimenter asking if they had liked the story and the one thing they liked best about it. Seven days later a forty item true-false test was given the pupils. Tests of significance showed that in every case the difference between the means of the groups was highly significant and always favored the high curiosity group.

The evidence from this study seems to indicate that children with a high level of curiosity either learn more in a given period of time, or they retain more of what they experienced. Perhaps the high curiosity children savor the story in their thinking and perhaps the details of it are more available to consciousness at the time of testing. It matters little whether there was more learning or greater retention. What is important is that children of comparable intelligence, but differing in curiosity, performed differently in the learning situation.

The usual school is one in which learners take part in a variety of activities over a relatively short period of time. If one were to look for a common element in many of these school experiences he would discover reading to be that element. This would surprise no one, since our schools employ the written word as a major means of communication and learning. It is, therefore, entirely proper to inquire as to whether curiosity has some influence on reading comprehension.

Using much the same procedure as in other studies, two groups were established to test the relationship between reading comprehension and high and low curiosity. The groups were matched on sex, race, popularity and intelligence. A Foolish Sayings Test was developed containing 22 items designed to measure the child's ability to sense important aspects of sentences. Some of the items in the test were common absurdities while others were straightforward statements. When the test results were analyzed it was found that the difference between means of the groups was significant beyond the .05 level (16). This leads to the interpretation that children with high curiosity tend to comprehend the meaning of sentences more accurately than do low curiosity children of equal intelligence.

From these studies it might be deduced that children with a high degree of curiosity move out from a familiar position and attempt to make contact with aspects of the environment that are novel. One might also deduce that children with low curiosity are prone to seek a balanced or homeostatic environment. Such was the basic position of a study (14) conducted to discover how varying degrees of curiosity in children affect their response to balanced and unbalanced stimuli. A group of high curiosity and low curiosity fifth grade students was established by using teacher judgments, peer judgments and self judgments of curiosity. To each child in both groups a test was then administered which measured his or her acceptance of the unbalanced and unfamiliar. The test was a paper-and-pencil instrument consisting of twenty pairs of geometric figures. One figure in each pair was more symmetrical and/or presumably more familiar than the other to the children. Comparison of the test means of the two groups indicated there was a difference significant at the .02 level. The evidence lends support to the idea that children of high curiosity select unbalanced and unfamiliar aspects of their environment more frequently than do fifth grade children having low curiosity.

Historically, educational research findings have had little impact on the educative process. One reason for this is that we are prone to discount the research because of its alleged sampling deficiencies, the inadequacy of the instruments used, or because it used subjects of one age group. With regard to the last criticism, the research on curiosity has dwelt mainly on the elementary age child, yet there are a few studies conducted in educational situations that have used high school or college students as subjects.

For example, Berlyne (8) used two groups of college freshmen and two groups of high school juniors to investigate the relation between uncertainty and curiosity. A series of 28 quotations, each one to two sentences in length, was put into a test booklet and students were told that prominent men in English or American literature had made the statements. Three alleged authors were given for each of the quotations but in no case was the true author's name one of those. The subjects were told that 100 high school teachers had read the quotes and indicated which of the three names given was the name of the true author. Each quote, therefore, had three authors' names after it, each followed by a number indicating how many teachers had chosen it. Uncertainty was introduced by virtue of the evenness or unevenness of distribution of the numbers that followed each author's name. Some quotes were designated *high-uncertainty quotations* because the distribution of teachers' choices was 34-33-33 (100 teachers); *medium uncertainty quotations* had a distribution of teacher choices that was 77-13-10; and, the *low uncertainty quotations* had a distribution of teacher choices that was 90-10. The quotations were read aloud, then the students were instructed to go back over the 28 quotations and mark the twelve whose true author they would most like to know. Then they were instructed to rank order the 12 selections they had made. For all 135 students who participated in the experiment the mean curiosity score for even-distribution (uncertainty) items was 2.98, while the mean curiosity score for uneven distribution quotations was 2.56. The difference in these means was significant at the .01 level. This suggests that curiosity increases with evenness of distribution of alleged teachers' guesses. In turn, it suggests that when alternatives approach the level of equaprobability there is greater uncertainty as to the response that an individual will make.

A teacher is prone to ask questions the answers to which could, conceivably, enable him to do a better job of teaching. The research on curiosity does not have immediate recommendations as to how the teacher may improve his instruction; yet certain techniques used in the conduct of research sometimes suggest ways in which teaching might be altered so as to improve learning of students. One such suggestion emerges from a study (4) which sought to determine the effects of pre-questioning on learning and curiosity. An experimental group of 24 high school biology students received a questionnaire about invertebrate animals prior to any other information about the animals. A control group did not receive the same fore-questionnaire. The 12 animals consisted of eight familiar and four unfamiliar of which two of the latter were fictitious. Following this, both the experimental and control groups were given 120 word paragraphs describing the animals (information input). After the word paragraphs had been read a 48 item test was given each subject. The test was constructed in such a way that the subjects answered either that they were certain of the answer from previous knowledge, or that they were surprised.

It was hypothesized that the experimental group would learn more effectively and would recall more answers than the control group, because their curiosity would be aroused by the fore-questionnaire. The findings support this hypothesis inasmuch as the experimental group made 32.41 correct responses on the post-test and the control group made 27.15 correct responses. The difference in these results was significant at the .01 level of probability. Apparently, the pre-questions did arouse curiosity and the surprising statements were more likely to be recalled as answers in the post-test than were other statements. One might say that the pre-questioning "tuned" the organism by arousing curiosity which, in turn, predisposed it toward acquisition of information.

One might take the position that curiosity is an inherent human factor and, therefore, that it should be manifest in varying degrees at all levels of intellectual ability. Conversely, one might argue that curiosity and intellectual ability are negatively correlated, and that low intelligence makes a person less sensitive to conflicting stimuli in his environment. The conflicting stimuli are the genesis of curiosity. Spitz and Hoats (25) contribute evidence that supports the latter point of view. Using a group of institutionalized high grade retardates, a group of equal chronological age normals and a group of equal mental age normals, they made comparisons as to "perceptual curiosity" of the subjects. The subjects were shown two patterns of a pair side by side for three seconds. One pattern of the pair was balanced and/or symmetrical or less irregular (LI), while the other pattern was more unbalanced and/or more irregular (MI). The subject was allowed after the three second viewing to press a button and to see, for as long as he chose, either pattern of the pair.

Thus, two scores were obtained, the pattern chosen and the length of time the chosen pattern was retained for viewing. There was a marked tendency for subjects to choose the less irregular over the more irregular patterns in all categories, even though there was variation among the groups. One of these variations was that normals, to a greater extent than the retardates, tended to look at complex stimuli relatively longer than at simpler stimuli.

Perhaps the findings of this study deviate from the findings of others because the methodology was different. Yet, it was not too different and, therefore, leads one to speculate as to why the retardates avoided the asymmetrical or uneven figures and apparently were more attracted to the redundant and balanced figures. It should be noted that balance rather than amount of information was the key factor in selection since each pattern of the pair contained the *same amount* of information but its arrangement was different. A brief excursion into the realm of "hunches" might suggest that the world of the retardate is one of relative chaos and complexity, and that his need therefore is to bring stability and balance into the picture. The work of Griffith, Spitz and Lipman (11) on the difficulty of the retardate in neatly categorizing incoming information is related to the idea already expressed.

Curiosity and Personality Variables

Someone, in describing children's learning, once said that children are not born anew on the doorsteps of the school each morning. Teachers need little reminding of this sage advice, for they are quick to recognize that, no matter the level of a child's intellect, or the opportunities present in the immediate classroom situation, a host of factors impinge upon the youngster and play a part in what he shall learn, when he shall learn it and how he shall learn it. Unfortunately, learning is not the simple act of taking over information that is made available, nor is teaching the simple act of organizing material in logical order and presenting it to learners.

It will be noted that in none of the studies reported has there been a description of personality variables that might influence curiosity and its role in learning as well as in general behavior. Many of the studies arouse curiosity by manipulation of different aspects of the environment such as card designs and flashing lights. Other studies have described how children with varying degrees of curiosity have performed on such things as reading comprehension, retention of learned material and stimulus ambiguity. It is patently clear that when a new avenue of research opens up—as in the case of curiosity—such research cannot proceed on all fronts at one and the same time. That is to say, the research must eventually touch on a variety of factors related to the central issue in order that a theory may be built, but it proceeds slowly, with one or a few factors at a time being investigated. The pieces of the puzzle are added slowly and not in one grand move. One can, however, speculate as to how other factors may eventually fit into the total picture. Indeed, there may even be research which is peripheral and yet related to the major issue. Such is the case with personality variables and their relation to curiosity.

It is not uncommon to hear teachers say that well adjusted children are usually the better learners. If this be true, one can say that curiosity in children is positively related to adequacy of adjustment. McReynolds and others (18) devised a study designed to test such a hypothesis. Thirty sixth grade children were rated by teachers as to their adjustment, and their curiosity scores were obtained by a special testing situation. Each child was asked to identify a number of objects by manipulating but not looking at the objects. A curiosity score was obtained by noting the amount of time the objects were manipulated. The correlations between psychological adjustment and object curiosity are as follows: overall psychological health and object curiosity .45; nervous behavior and object curiosity —.42; worry over achievement and object curiosity —.27; maladjustment in the classroom and object curiosity —.50; maladjustment to teacher and object curiosity —.42; maladjustment to peers and object curiosity —.39; and scholastic motivation and object curiosity .43. These results raise the possibility that those aspects of the classroom learning situation which depend upon curiosity are hindered by anxieties of the pupil. While the correlations are not particularly high, there is a pattern having to do with the social context of the classroom that cannot be ignored. Specifically, we refer to the negative correlations between curiosity and maladjustment in the classroom, maladjustment to teacher and maladjustment to peers. Generalizing, there is a negative correlation between curiosity and various aspects of social relationships in the class-room.

In previous descriptions of research it has been shown that new, novel or different situations are found to be related to the curiosity aroused. Yet all new situations may not be of the type that engender curiosity in all individuals. Again, we are confronted with the notion that a person's psychological adjustment may have some influence on the way in which he reacts to strange situations. Such might be the case when a child is brought to a center for a mental, dental or physical examination. Shirley (21) devised a scoring system to assess responses made by children upon departing from home and arriving at a social service center for some type of examination. The scoring system was an eight point hierarchy ranging from a child's crying and refusing to leave the mother to his departing from home and arriving at the center eagerly. The author summarized by stating that a child's level of adjustment to the experience at the center depended little upon the features of the day and little upon his health. Adjustment to the center appeared to be much more dependent upon wholesomeness of upbringing in the home and upon the security given by parents. This study did not deal directly with curiosity but it does suggest that a child's security influences the degree to which new or strange situations are welcomed or dreaded.

We have found that subjects, with few exceptions, give greater attention to and are more curious about stimuli that are incongruous, ambiguous or novel. When psychological stress enters into the situation, the results are much less clear-cut. If stress is introduced, one might hypothesize that ambiguity is intolerable to the individual and that he will give a definite response (closure) to a stimulus configuration before he has adequate information to make the correct response (23). Stress in this case would tend to strengthen the "hypotheses" that a person has about his environment and he would need little data to confirm the hypotheses even though they may result in incorrect responses. Test of this idea was made by using a series of 15 cards, beginning with an ambiguous card but with additional elements being added with each succeeding card until the complete picture or design emerged on the last card of the series. The subjects were asked to give the correct response as soon as they could, that is, on as few cards as possible. The test was given to one group under stressful conditions and to another group under security conditions. There were generally significant differences between the stress and security groups on the test. This generalized finding suggests that psychological stress results in premature closure (early incorrect answers) and a tendency to adhere to one's expectancies (pre-recognition hypotheses) in ambiguous task situations. Stress or anxiety results in cognitive and perceptual processes that preserve a familiar behavioral and perceptual field for the individual. A familiar behavioral and perceptual field would *not* arouse conflicting aspects of the field which in turn would not arouse curiosity.

The role of anxiety in novelty-seeking behavior (curiosity) has been investigated by Haywood (12). Twenty subjects at each of three levels of manifest anxiety (low, moderate, high) had to choose between the novel and familiar members of 15 pairs of stimulus cards before and after a taped presentation of an incomprehensible message. Measures of palmar sweating were taken immediately following each of the two novelty-seeking tests. A control group went through the same procedure except that the arousal message was omitted. Novelty-seeking scores were the number of novel cards chosen out of 15 choices and the mean number of seconds spent viewing the novel cards. All three experimental groups exhibited a decrease (P <.01) in mean number of novel stimulus cards chosen for viewing following the arousal message, while the control group actually increased in this measure of novelty-seeking. Palmar sweating increased significantly (P <.005) with imposition of the arousal message in all experimental groups. This means that when anxiety was aroused, the tendency was for subjects to seek less novelty. Translating this into a classroom situation, it could be said that as a child's anxiety is aroused he will be less receptive to new curricular content which is made available to him. These findings agree with those of Sarason (20).

The major intent of this section has been to present evidence about curiosity and personality correlates. Admittedly, some of the evidence presented is somewhat peripheral while some of it is of a more central nature. The author succumbs to a strong temptation to cite one final bit of peripheral evidence by harking the reader back to a study cited (7) in an earlier section of this paper. The study was somewhat contradictory to others done in a similar way in the sense that subjects did not always seek the more irregular choices in pair of patterns. Rather, it was found there was a decided tendency for subjects to make preponderantly less irregular or preponderantly more irregular choices. The distribution was, therefore, bimodal. This biomodality of choices may reflect personality differences.

It will be recalled that Barron and Welsh (1) used a figure preference test to ascertain whether perception was a possible factor in personality style. Their major finding was that personality differences are linked with preferences for complexity or simplicity. This might mean that some people have personality styles in which simplicity, order and organization are fundamental. On the other hand, other individuals may have personality styles in which complexity, ambiguity and relative disorder are fundamental. Curiosity is a dynamic that functions because of the input of data, but it must be remembered that the self is the data processor of the organism acting on the data in a selective fashion.

References

1. F. Barron and G. S. Welsh. "Perception as a Possible Factor in Personality Style: Its Measurement by a Figure Preference Test." *Journal of Psychology* 33: 199-207; 1952.

2. D. E. Berlyne. "Novelty and Curiosity as Determinants of Exploratory Behavior." *British Journal of Psychology* 41: 68-80; 1950.

3. D. E. Berlyne. "Attention to Change." *British Journal of Psychology* 42 (3): 269-78; 1951.

4. D. E. Berlyne. "An Experimental Study of Human Curiosity." *British Journal of Psychology* 45 (4): 256-65; November 1954.

5. D. E. Berlyne. "Conflict and Information—Theory Variables as Determinants of Human Perceptual Curiosity." *Journal of Experimental Psychology* 53 (6): 399-404; June 1957.

6. D. E. Berlyne. "Influence of Complexity and Novelty in Visual Figures on Orienting Responses." *Journal of Experimental Psychology* 55 (3): 289-96; 1958.

7. D. E. Berlyne. *Conflict, Arousal, and Curiosity.* New York: McGraw-Hill Book Company, 1960.

8. D. E. Berlyne. "Uncertainty and Epistemic Curiosity." *British Journal of Psychology* 53 (1): 27-34; 1962.

9. D. E. Berlyne. "Complexity and Incongruity as Determinants of Exploratory Choice and Evaluative Ratings." Unpublished mimeographed paper, 1963. 14 p.

10. Murray Glanzer. "Curiosity, Exploratory Drive and Stimulus Satiation." *Psychological Bulletin* 55 (5): 302-15; 1958.

11. B. C. Griffith, H. H. Spitz and R. S. Lipman. "Verbal Mediation and Concept Formation in Retarded and Normal Subjects." *Journal of Experimental Psychology* 58: 247-51; 1959.

12. H. C. Haywood. Veterans Administration Hospital, Danville, Illinois. "Arousal, Novelty Seeking and Palmar Sweat." Unpublished research report filed with Veterans Administration. 1961.

12a. W. H. Maw and E. W. Maw. "Relationship Between Curiosity and Scores on a Test of General Information." *Association for Research in Growth Relationships* 1: 27-32; 1960.

13. W. H. Maw and E. W. Maw. "Information Recognition by

Children with High and Low Curiosity." *Educational Research Bulletin* 40 (8): 197-201; November 1961.

14. W. H. Maw and E. W. Maw. "Nonhomeostatic Experiences as Stimuli of Children with High Curiosity." *California Journal of Educational Research* 12 (2): 57-61; March 1961.

15. W. H. Maw and E. W. Maw. "Establishing Criterion Groups for Evaluation Measures of Curiosity." *Journal of Experimental Education* 29 (3): 299-305; March 1961.

16. W. H. Maw and E. W. Maw. "Children's Curiosity as an Aspect of Reading Comprehension." *The Reading Teacher* 15 (4): 236-40; January 1962.

17. W. H. Maw and E. W. Maw. "Selection of Unbalanced and Unusual Designs by Children High in Curiosity." *Child Development* 33 (4): 917-22; December 1962.

18. Paul McReynolds, Mary Acker and Carol Pietila. "Relation of Object Curiosity to Psychological Adjustment in Children." *Child Development* 32 (2): 393-400; June 1961.

19. Leon R. Mittman and Glenn Terrell. "An Experimental Study of Curiosity in Children." Unpublished paper read at Society for Research and Child Development; April 1963.

20. Seymour Sarason, *et al. Anxiety in Elementary School Children.* New York: John Wiley & Sons, 1960.

21. M. M. Shirley. "Children's Adjustment to a Strange Situation." *Journal of Abnormal and Social Psychology* 37: 201-17; 1942.

22. C. D. Smock. "The Influence of Psychological Stress on the Intolerance of Ambiguity." *Journal of Abnormal and Social Psychology* 50: 177-82; 1955.

23. C. D. Smock. "The Influence of Stress on the Perception of Incongruity." *Journal of Abnormal and Social Psychology* 50: 354-56; 1955.

24. C. D. Smock and Bess G. Holt. "Children's Reactions to Novelty: An Experimental Study of Curiosity Motivation." *Child Development* 33: 631-42; 1962.

25. H. H. Spitz and D. L. Hoats. "Experiments on Perceptual Curiosity Behavior in Mental Retardates." Final report on NIMH M-4533. Bordentown, New Jersey: E. R. Johnstone Training and Research Center, 1961.

26. P. Solomon. *Sensory Deprivation.* Cambridge: Harvard University Press, 1961.

27. W. L. Welker. "Some Determinants of Play and Exploration in Chimpanzees." *Journal of Comparative Physiological Psychology* 49: 84-89; 1956.

28. Jack Wertheim and S. A. Mednick. "The Achievement Motive and Field Independence." *Journal of Consulting Psychology* 22 (1): 38; 1958.

29. Robert Woodward. *Dynamics of Behavior.* New York: Henry Holt & Company, 1958.

The Child and the Inquiry Process

J. Richard Suchman

MAN'S ability to understand and control his environment depends on how well he has conceptualized it—how closely his conceptual systems correspond to reality. When one person tries to shape the concepts of another by talking to him or showing him something or giving him something to read, we call it teaching. When a person tries to promote these conceptual changes for himself by gathering and processing information, the activity becomes inquiry.

If man could not inquire, he could not gather and process data, raise and test hypotheses, build theories and test them empirically; all of his learning would have to be programed for him by others. Data would have to be fed to him, inferences would have to be drawn for him, and he would have to be told at every turn what conclusions could be drawn. In short, he would be totally dependent as a learner and a thinker. It is obvious therefore that being able to inquire is a necessary condition for the independence and autonomy of learning.

Inquiry is a fundamental form of learning. Long before the child begins formal education he is gathering data from his environment. The infant grasps a pot, picks it up, feels it, turns it over, puts blocks in it, dumps them out, and so forth. These interactions with the environment help to form intuitive schemata by which the child begins to internalize the properties of his environment.

Assimilation and Accommodation

As he grows older, the child learns to become more systematic in his searching and in his collection and processing of data. As his conceptual

59

systems become broader and more complex, the methods by which he acquires and organizes data become more sophisticated. As a result he is able to build more elaborate and accurate conceptual structures which reflect more closely the complexities of the real world.

In analyzing the act of inquiry it is helpful to think in terms of two basic processes. The first of these consists of taking in and incorporating what we perceive in terms of what we know and understand. We process data in terms of our conceptual systems. A child sees an object that has a wooden handle and a long metal blade attached to it. It looks to him very much like a knife. We can say that the child has assimilated his perception of the object in terms of a well established conceptual system related to knives. The process of assimilation goes on continuously as we encounter familiar objects, events and situations. As long as we have the appropriate conceptual categories and models, there is no conflict, and assimilation occurs without difficulty.

Supposing that when the object is held over a flame, the blade bends downward. If the child has had experience with objects that melt and slump downward as the result of melting, he can apply this model to the perceived event and still can *assimilate* this experience. Next we plunge the blade into a tank of water whereupon it straightens out to its original shape. Then we place the blade back over the flame in an inverted position, and this time it bends upward instead of downward. If the perceiver is a sixth grade child, it is very likely that this experience will come as something of a shock. He is now confronted by a *discrepant event,* one which he could not have predicted and is not able to explain within the framework of his existing conceptual models. He faces a dilemma in the form of an experience which he cannot *assimilate.* Moreover, before he is able to assimilate this experience he will have to learn more about the properties of the blade and the circumstances under which the bending took place. He may have to create a new conceptual model by combining parts of old models. If he has no teacher to engineer this conceptual reorganization for him through explanation and demonstration, he will have to do this for himself by experimenting and gathering data, by trying out various combinations of conceptual models, and testing each of these experimentally until he finally arrives at a point where he has a model that seems to match the event.

This process of reshaping and reorganizing conceptual structures until they fit and account for perceived events is known as *accommodation.* Inquiry involves both assimilation and accommodation in complementary roles. The inquirer, faced with a discrepant event, may first attempt to break it down into component parts, to analyze it in terms of variables which he has already conceptualized. In the case of the knife that is not a knife (it is actually a bimetallic strip), he may try to find out what the blade is made of or how it is put together. He may try to determine the changing temperature of the blade or the temperature of the water in the tank. He may wonder about the size and shape of the blade and try to find out more about changes in these conditions throughout the observed event. Through the process of analysis he may have obtained enough information about the event to assimilate it entirely. If he is aware of the fact that metals expand with increases in temperature, and the fact that two different metals may expand at different rates, and if, in addition, he discovers that the blade is made of two different metals welded together, he may arrive at the hypothesis that the bending was caused by stresses produced by the differential expansion within the blade. Analysis of this kind paves the way for conceptual reorganization. Yet before the child is able to assimilate the event, he must pull together the results of his analysis. To these analyzed data he tries to apply various combinations of explanatory conceptual models until he has constructed one that seems to account for what he has perceived. Accommodation provides for the necessary restructuring of concepts that enables the child to assimilate formerly discrepant events.

Through the dual processes of assimilation and accommodation a person is able to build theories, test them, incorporate them within a broader conceptual system and use them in finding greater meaning and unity in experience.

Inquiry in Contrast to Engineered Learning

It is possible for a teacher to engineer conceptual reorganization in a child and to bring about the child's accommodation to discrepant events by programing a series of experiences, by drawing on past experiences, and by focusing attention through verbal instruction and exposition on selected aspects of his environment. In order to be effective in doing this, however, it is important for a teacher to be reasonably well acquainted with the existing conceptual structures of the learner and to keep a constant check on the conceptual modifications that are taking place at every step along the way. This is very difficult even when the teacher-pupil ratio is one-to-one. It of course becomes more difficult as the number of pupils increases.

When the mode of learning is inquiry, however, the process of data gathering, analysis and experimentation is under the control of the learner himself. He is free to reach out in whatever direction he chooses for data and to gather this information in whatever sequence is most meaningful to him. Through inquiry, the learner influences and actually programs his own learning in terms of his own cognitive needs as dictated by his style of learning and his informational needs of the moment.

To summarize thus far, inquiry can be regarded as a fundamental learning process, which is under the autonomous control of the learner and promotes conceptual growth through the dual and complementary functions of assimilation and accommodation.

Developmental Changes in Inquiry

The course of development of thinking, as described by Inhelder and Piaget (1958), moves from the highly egocentric, intuitive and concrete toward the more decentralized, analytical and abstract. There is no mode of mental activity in which these developmental trends are more evident than the process of inquiry. At a very early age this process is seen as taking the form of sensorimotor learning. This is the seemingly disorganized interaction with the environment through which the child builds a repertoire of intuitive schemata representing the properties of his environment. These schemata are by-products of his attempts to manipulate and control his environment. Later, during the preschool years, data gathering takes on a somewhat more organized form. This stage is called "pre-operational" because the child is still concerned with producing an effect rather than seeing a relationship. As yet he is unable to see his manipulations as tentative and reversible. He does not regard them as operations that can be done and undone or as experiments that can be replicated.

Once the child crosses over into operational thinking, his inquiry takes on more of the character of research. He can subdivide his activity into separate operations and can examine the effects of each operation independently from that which precedes or follows it. He is therefore able to experiment in a somewhat controlled fashion. At first he performs only concrete operations, that is, he manipulates the environment directly and groups his findings in ways that are likely to yield new ideas and conceptual organizations. In looking for an explanation of the bimetal strip, he might try varying the temperature first in one direction and then in another and observing the consequences of these changes. From this information, he might hypothesize a systematic relationship between temperature and the bending of the blade.

As the child approaches adolescence he becomes capable of going beyond concrete operations to the point where he can manipulate ideas and propositions and test hypotheses through formal logical operations. Thus, while the child at the stage of concrete operations might discover through the manipulation of materials that a bimetal strip will bend only when two different metals are used, the adolescent who has arrived at the level of formal logical operations might be able to deduce this same conclusion logically:

The metals must bend because they are fixed to each other along a common surface. The area of one becomes greater than the area of the other because they expand at different rates. Some internal stress must be produced. The only configuration that would permit the common surface to remain unchanged while one metal becomes larger than the other would be that of concentric circles.

The formal logical process by which the adult arrives at the conclusion that the blade had to bend seems far removed from the almost random exploratory manipulations of the infant, but they are both forms of inquiry because the learner increases his understanding of his environment through *self-directed* actions. There are many important changes in the way the autonomy of the learner is translated into plans and actions, into strategies and schemata. The infant centers on objects and comes to sense their properties intuitively by playing with them. The older child seeks to control the objects of his environment and learns how his manipulations as causes correlate with outcomes as effects. In time he abstracts from observed relationships concepts of causality. Perhaps it is more accurate to say that he constructs or invents these conceptual models of causality. Yet they are shaped by the events that he creates through his operations. He produces the data he needs in shaping, trying out, testing and revising his conceptual models of the real world. The mature mind can go one step further and test the validity of a construct or test a hypothesis logically, and completely bypass certain empirical or concrete operations.

Motivation of Inquiry

Throughout these changes in the *form* of inquiry, its motivational basis is subject to very little change. The motivation to inquire is rooted partly in the need to assimilate perceived objects and events. At all levels of inquiry we pursue meaning, that is, we seek to relate new experience to old conceptual structures. Regardless of the level of sophistication that the pursuit takes, the activity of gathering and processing information is exciting and pleasurable. The ability to assimilate discrepant events is intrinsically rewarding, and the construction of new conceptual models that enable one to find new meaning in old events creates in the learner a sense of power. These are satisfactions that result from the act of inquiring or its immediate consequences and serve to motivate learning when it occurs in the inquiry mode.

One of the by-products of recent investigations dealing with new methods of instruction in science, mathematics, and social studies has been the almost universal recognition by the researchers of a kind of motivation that was not found in the traditional learning situation.

Bruner (1961) has been one of the most articulate in describing this phenomenon. These new teaching methods have all involved the more or less inductive approach in which new understandings come to light through a form of discovery by the individual learner. It was sensed by Bruner and others that the act of discovery had a number of highly desirable consequences not the least of which was a high level of motivation. He noted that discovery tended to produce much activity and interest, a sense of intellectual potency in the learner, an increasing faith in the regularity of the universe. This faith seemed to promote a feeling of confidence in the child that prompted him to pursue his learning activities in search of more and more of these regularities.

Just what is discovery? Is it a highly creative act that involves the sudden recognition of something very new and unique? Or is it simply the recognition of order in what formerly appeared to be chaos? The term is used in a great many ways so that now it seems to be unwise to use it to describe any particular cognitive act. Yet the sense of discovery, the "aha" feeling does seem to turn up only under certain circumstances. It seems to happen only when assimilation is finally achieved after it is first blocked. When the discrepant event is suddenly rendered assimilable through cognitive reorganization there is a release of tension and a feeling of satisfaction.

Here then is reward that is directly associated with the process of inquiry. So long as a child can believe that a new discovery can result from inquiry, he will inquire without any outside pressure to do so.

Yet is there a motivation entirely *intrinsic in the act* of inquiry itself? Is the expectation of closure a necessary condition for the motivation of search? Hunt (1962) suggests yet another motivating force. He calls it the "motivation inherent in information processing and action." What he is saying in effect is that we have a need for cognitive activity, a need that can be met only by the intake of data, the processing of it, the drawing of inferences from it and the making of decisions. Another way of saying this might be that we have the need to inquire, not because inquiry leads to the joyous experience of discovery but simply because inquiry itself is a highly satisfying and stimulating activity.

One may then raise the question that if Hunt is right, why do we not find our schools filled with inquirers gathering data and satisfying this need? One answer may be that inquiry would be the dominant mode of learning in the school except that we have done a highly effective job of preventing this from taking place by utilizing ego and social needs to motivate children to conform rather than to inquire, to store facts and generalizations rather than to search and discover for themselves. Perhaps it has been that by providing a climate hostile to inquiry we have succeeded in preventing this motivational force from promoting inquiry activity and permitting children to develop the skills of inquiry and the attitudes that lead to its use.

Alpert (1960) has addressed himself to the problem of motivating curiosity in the schools. He suggests that we do this by utilizing the child's dependency on the teacher for social support. According to his plan the teacher acts toward the child *as though* the child is a curious person. The purpose is to shape the child's self-concept so that he comes to see himself as curious and then begins to take on curious behavior to correspond with this new self-image.

The theoretical implications of such an approach are most interesting. Can one expect a person to become curious because he has come to see himself as a curious person? Can we get a child to alter his self-image simply by giving social reinforcement to a new image? Will any resulting behavior change persist when the teacher is no longer around to reinforce the new self-image? We do not have answers to these questions, but it does seem that a more direct approach to promoting curiosity in anybody is to confront him with an event or object that is *discrepant enough to make him curious*—to build up irresistible pressures in the child to find a way of assimilating the event. As Bruner and others point out, the child who attains new understandings for himself gains a sense of intellectual power (Bruner, 1961), mastery (White, 1959), or accomplishment (Erikson, 1950). The new self-image that results grows out of what the child knows he has actually done. He sees himself as a curious person and an autonomous inquirer because he *has been* curious and autonomous. Once this image is established it is likely to promote more of the same kind of behavior.

Inquiry and Cognitive Style

The element of autonomy that characterizes inquiry has special psychological significance for conceptual growth because it allows the learner to adapt the learning process to his immediate cognitive needs. These needs are in part a function of the way the learner thinks. Each learner has a style of conceptualization which strongly influences the mode by which he gathers, processes and uses data. In other words, because inquiry is a self-directed mode of learning, it permits the learner to adapt the process of learning to match his own particular style of thinking.

Jerome Kagan at the Fels Research Institute and Irving Sigel at the Merrill-Palmer Institute have sampled these styles through a variety of instruments designed to reflect the basis upon which a subject prefers to associate elements of his perceived environment. They have been able to distinguish two and possibly three fundamental styles. These styles can best be illustrated by a sample test item. A child a presented with a card on which appear three pictures—a garden, a rake and a fork. The child is asked to pick the two pictures that seem to go together and to give the reason for associating these two. If the child picks the rake and the garden because a rake is used in a garden, he is relying on past associations. He is linking together entities which have been contiguous in his experience. This style is called "relational" because linkages are made on the basis of directly observed relationships and do not require the use of conceptual systems or abstractions. The relational thinker does not stray too far from his perceptions and the associations that have grown out of them.

If the child says that the fork and the rake go together because they both have tines, he is making his association on the basis of a breakdown of perceived wholes into meaningful components. This style is called "descriptive-analytical" because the associations are formed through the analysis of experience. He has linked the fork and the rake on the basis of a component characteristic of each of them which he was able to respond to only because he had first dissociated the parts of both objects and then compared them in terms of one or more of these parts. The relational thinker is more likely to rely heavily on impressions while the analytical thinker tends to reflect on his percepts within a systematic framework of conceptual categories.

Kagan, Sigel and Moss (1961) found these styles to have consistency within individuals over time and over a wide range of cognitive tasks. Boys tend to be more analytical than girls, and both become less relational and more analytical with age.

These styles affect the inquiry process. Children show inquiry strategies that correspond to these cognitive styles. A study by Suchman and Kagan, not yet published, found that children with highly analytical styles of thinking tended to inquire more analytically, gathering data primarily for the purpose of analysis. The relational (low analytical) children were more inclined to form hypotheses based on impressions, bypassing the analytical process. The children selected inquiry strategies that best suited their styles of thinking. Further investigations of the relationship between cognitive styles and inquiry are now in progress.

Inquiry and Conceptual Growth

It is well-known that you can get a child to become aware of a relationship or principle by exposing him to enough situations where the principle is operant. In time he will abstract the concept or generalize over the experiences. If the instances are carefully selected, one can guide or engineer the discovery of new relationships. Beberman's (1958) and

Hendrix's (1961) approach to teaching algebra is based on this. They take the position that there is little point in talking about, let us say, the commutative principle unless the pupils have almost an intuitive understanding of just what the principle is. Too often when this is taught through a verbal didactic method, the pupils acquire merely a superficial, mechanistic understanding. They know what they have to do to get the answer but they do not know *why*. Beberman's method literally engineers the students into discovering the principle themselves. His pupils are given a series of mathematical operations to perform which can be done with simple arithmetic. The problems are arranged in order of increasing difficulty in that the numbers get larger and more difficult to handle arithmetically. However, it is possible to discover a short-cut that simplifies the calculation. By discovering this short-cut, the pupil has discovered the algebraic principle.

Without the benefit of a carefully programed set of experiences, one must go through a less-directed series of operations to arrive at a given concept. Before arriving at such a concept one might have to construct a number of intermediate and inadequate solutions in a succession of conceptual reorganizations. Is there any advantage in such trial and error thinking?

Smedslund (1961) wondered about this and tried to determine whether the emerging concept is different in the one case in which it results from a simple generalization drawn from a set of positive instances and in the other case in which it is the end product of a series of conceptual reorganizations. He worked with preschool children and used the concept of the conservation of weight. He got one group of children to discover empirically that the weight of a plasticene ball does not change as its shape is modified. He contrasted this with another group whose members had come to internalize the concept of the conservation of weight through the natural processes by which such concepts become internalized (Piaget, 1941). He found that concepts that are easily formed by simple generalizations are more readily discarded when data are discrepant to the concept. But when the concepts result from the resolution of conflicts in successive accommodations as in the normal course of conceptual growth, a conceptual structure is not easily given up even in the face of a heavy weight of discrepant data. Smedslund sneaked a little piece of clay away from the plasticene ball so that the children would not know he had done this. He then changed the shape of the ball and weighed it for the children so that they could see that its weight had changed as the shape was changed. Those children who had formed the concept of the conservation of weight simply through the generalization over several positive instances were quite ready to give up this concept in the face of *one discrepant event*. The other group, however, refused to accept the data as valid and raised rather strong doubts as to the honesty of the experimenter presenting the demonstration.

This suggests certain weaknesses in any learning situation in which the conceptual increments toward each new structure are pre-programed for speed and ease of learning. It almost seems that when conceptual structures are formed by outside agents that obviate the learner's own accommodative struggles, the new concept is not hard-won or self-structured. It is less a part of the learner, less useful to him (Festinger, 1957). He is therefore more willing to relinquish the concept if new data challenge its validity.

The step-by-step path toward conceptual growth is typical of most teacher-directed learning. The primary objective is the attainment of a new concept. This attainment is engineered by starting with the familiar and moving with or without discovery toward the unfamiliar with the purpose of assimilating this in the framework of existing structures. The assumption is that all learners begin with conceptual structures and cognitive styles that are enough alike to permit a standard sequence of operations (or lesson plan) to bring them to the same level of conceptualization.

Yet children's conceptual models differ enormously in structure. Take the relatively simple phenomenon of floating bodies. What makes an air bubble rise to the surface of a liquid? Some children have very diffuse notions that involve the "lightness of air" or the "tendency for gases to rise." Some believe that water pressure has something to do with it and that water pressure acts only in a downward direction. Some children understand the depth-pressure relationships in liquids, but fail to see this at all as related to gravity.

If a child is going to reorganize his concepts of floating or sinking, he will have to be able to proceed from where he is and not from some hypothetical point of ignorance. He must have the opportunity to try out his conceptual models by using them to design experiments and make predictions. He must be free to gather the data he needs to resolve his cognitive conflicts until he has evolved a conceptual system that lets him assimilate what he sees. In short, a realistic approach to conceptual growth must allow the learner to gather and process data in accordance with his cognitive needs of the moment, and this suggests he should be utilizing some form of inquiry.

Means of Promoting Inquiry

There is a wide range of cognitive skills involved in the inquiry process. This includes the gathering, organizing and processing of data, the trying out of conceptual models, the restructuring of these models to accommodate to new data, and the testing of models for validity. At times it is necessary to use exacting methods of sampling, control and analysis. At other times a wild intuitive leap might be the operation most needed. There are broad strategies and special tactics that help to make inquiry more productive. The one most dependable characteristic of inquiry is that there is no one fixed method of operation. To build and strengthen inquiry skills, one would be hard-put in trying to identify a set of specific component skills that would have to be independently exercised and strengthened. Even if it were possible to make children more perceptive or flexible by giving them special exercises in this kind of activity, it is very doubtful whether such a piecemeal approach would make a significant difference in the inquiry of children.

The element of creativity seems to play an important role in the inquiry process. Both in searching for new data and in restructuring conceptual systems to accommodate to new data the inquirer must act creatively. Torrance (1962), Getzels and Jackson (1962), and Guilford (1952) have made notable advances in identifying the conditions that appear to affect the creative process. Torrance lists the following conditions as necessary "for the healthy functioning of the preconscious mental processes which produce creativity":

1. The absence of serious threat to the self, the willingness to risk

2. Self-awareness—in touch with one's feelings

3. Self-differentiation—sees self as being different from others

4. Both openness to the ideas of others and confidence in one's own perceptions of reality or in one's own ideas

5. Mutuality in interpersonal relations—balance between excessive quest for social relations and pathological rejection of them.

These conditions seem to center about the ego and suggest that creativity increases as the ego is freed from inhibition and external domination, yet stays open to the intake of ideas from the outside.

Getzels and Jackson lend further support to the notion that creativity is promoted more through environmental conditions than through specific training. I quote from their book:

> Without passing premature judgment on the possibility of some positive effects from special instruction, we hold that boldness in thinking, free reign to the imagination, and creativity in performance will not be easily coming through piecemeal lessons and artificial stimulants. What is needed is a change in the entire intellectual climate in which we—the parents and the teachers—as well as the children function.

The findings of these researches point to the significance of attitudes and climates. They speak of the positive effects of "intellectual playfulness on creativity." Quoting again:

The relevant educational issue might well be: Are there certain areas of instruction in which opportunities are provided for "discovering" as well as for "remembering"? Is there provision in the curriculum for playing with facts and ideas as well as for repeating them? Can we teach students to be more sensitive to the nature of problems? Can we teach them that a problem may have several different interpretations and solutions? Even if there is only one right answer as in a mathematics problem, can a student solve the problem in a number of different ways?

The build-up of a given set of response patterns is a lot simpler to achieve than the promotion of creative thinking. In the case of the former, high pressure through strong and repeated reinforcements will generally have the desired effect. But high pressure has a way of interfering with creativity in forcing children to rely on stereotyped behavior. Creativity seems to occur most readily under conditions of low pressure.

One aspect of climate received extensive treatment in the research of Bruner *et al.* (1958) as reported in *A Study of Thinking.* One of the more significant outcomes of these studies was the identification of several search and concept attainment strategies and the recognition of the fact that the kinds of strategies used by the subjects were determined in part by the "pay-off matrix." That is, the way the subjects went about gathering data was largely a function of the kinds of performances that were being rewarded. When speed was rewarded, the subjects took greater risks and adopted a gambling strategy to save time. They leaped in to test hypotheses that had a far less than 50-50 chance of being valid. They also started testing hypotheses after they had gathered only a small proportion of the available data. But when the time pressure was off and accuracy and economy of operations were made the important criteria for success, the strategy shifted. Stress on the economy of operations encouraged some to try to retain a maximum amount of data in their heads, although cognitive strain of this kind was generally avoided. When freedom from error was an important success criterion, the subjects took a slower but safer route.

These findings suggest that inquiry strategies are flexible and can be adjusted to the demands of the problem situation. The so-called "scientific method" is not a fixed sequence of operations such as (a) "define the problem," (b) "formulate hypotheses," and (c) "gather data," etc. Scientists have reported that *their* methods vary widely according to *their* problems, just as the strategies of Bruner's subjects do.

MacKinnon (1961) also found no set patterns in the searching and thinking of highly creative architects and engineers. He concluded that:

If the widest possible relationships among facts are to be established, if what I would call the structure of knowledge is to be grasped, it is necessary that the student have a large body of facts which he has learned, as well as a

70

large array of reasoning skills which he has mastered. . . . A knowledgeable person in science is not merely one who has an accumulation of facts, but rather one who has the capacity to have sport with what he knows, giving creative rein to his fancy in changing his world of phenomenal appearances into a world of scientific constructs.

Bearing in mind that the process of inquiry has a large creative component, yet cannot depart from the realm of logic and reason, we shall turn now to the problem of developing inquiry in the elementary school.

The Inquiry Training Project

The Inquiry Training Project (Suchman, 1960, 1961, 1962) came into being because it seemed that the process of inquiry is basic to all intellectual activity, and because our pilot studies showed that elementary school children at the level of the intermediate grades did not seem to be either willing or able to inquire productively even when they were faced with events that aroused their curiosity. When they did make attempts to obtain closure, these attempts were highly dependent in the sense that the children merely asked for explanations. Apparently they had been accustomed to having their conceptual growth engineered for them by teachers and did not know how to achieve this autonomously by asking questions to gather information.

Although it has been modified in many ways since the time of its inception in 1957, Inquiry Training still retains the same basic form with which it started. The children work as a group. A concrete problem is posed in the form of a motion picture film of a physics demonstration. This film is designed to puzzle the children. The event is not one which an elementary school child would easily explain simply by observing. Many of the critical variables, the nature of the materials used, the conditions of the materials and the changes in these conditions are not observable in the film and must be verified in other ways.

The children are asked to find out why the events in the filmed episode occurred. The problem posed to them is one of constructing an explanatory system. In order to gather the information that they need they must ask questions. We restrict them to questions that can be answered by "yes" or "no" to prevent them from falling back into the open-ended type of inquiry in which the responsibility for structuring is in the teacher's hands. The yes-or-no question forces the children to think through and structure their own questions.

Inquiry sessions last between 30 and 60 minutes and each one is based on a different problem film. In structuring the inquiry sessions we try to provide the following three conditions:

1. *A problem that is real and meaningful to the children,* a discrepant event that they are unable to assimilate because: (a) they have not fully analyzed the event in terms of all the relevant variables, and (b) because they do not have the necessary conceptual models to assimilate the event in the way that they initially perceive it. The problem therefore is one of having to analyze and accommodate before assimilation can take place.

2. The second condition is the *freedom* given the children to gather whatever data they want in whatever sequence they desire. No attempt is made to guide or program the data given to the children beyond what is presented within the film itself. This condition allows the individual child to search in whatever direction he wants in gathering data to satisfy his own cognitive needs.

3. The third condition is *a responsive environment.* We attempt to provide the information asked for by the children as promptly and as accurately as possible so that the inquiry process is not blocked by delays or frustrations.

No external reinforcements or pressures are built into the program. Inquiry is motivated primarily by the satisfactions intrinsic in the process itself. Part of this, we believe, is gained through the progress the children make toward greater understanding of the problem episode. The other part of the motivation comes from the excitement inherent in gathering and processing data. Of course, one cannot keep out ego and social motivation. Children ask questions to impress other children with what they know, and many are driven by the need to have the satisfaction of finding the "right answer." However, the teacher tries to protect the children from these and other extrinsic pressures to allow the satisfaction to grow out of the activities themselves and not to have it artificially generated by outside agents.

The inquiry sessions enable the children to learn some of the effects of various strategies of data gathering and processing. However, this awareness of the dimensions of the inquiry process and the logical structures that are used in the construction of explanatory systems can be developed more rapidly and effectively if the children's attention is brought back to the process of inquiry itself after they are no longer engaged in the science problem. A "critique" is given as a follow-up of the inquiry session. A tape recording of the inquiry session is played back to the children so that the group can observe the effects of various types and groupings of questions. In examining and evaluating their own question asking, the children are able to see many of the dimensions of strategy.

The inquiry sessions and the follow-up critique sessions fulfill the major requirements of Inquiry Training. The children have a series of experiences in attempting to construct explanatory models for observed events and have a way of reviewing, examining and analyzing their previous inquiries so that they can be more effective and planful in future inquiry sessions.

In the academic year of 1960-61, we conducted an experiment to determine the effects of Inquiry Training over a 24-week period (Suchman, 1962). Twelve teachers were especially trained over the summer and each week during the experiment they spent an hour providing Inquiry Training for a full classroom of children. Each school that had an Inquiry Training group also had a control group. The control groups were given the same science content through the same films used to pose the Inquiry Training problems, but no practice or critiques relating to inquiry itself were given.

Evaluation of Inquiry Training posed a problem. None of the standardized aptitude or achievement tests could measure the kinds of changes Inquiry Training effects in the children. Of special concern were the changes in the inquiry process itself, in the willingness and ability of the children to gather data autonomously and to attempt to build explanatory models on their own. There was interest too in conceptual growth, not in how many facts and generalizations the children had stored and could report verbally, but in the actual change in the children's internalized structure of physical relationships.

We had to devise our own instruments and it was this problem that gave the study some of its biggest headaches. To measure these two kinds of outcomes, we constructed two very different kinds of tests.

The analysis of the inquiry process could only be based on a sample of the child's inquiry. The "Questest" was designed to obtain just such a sample. Special problem films were used. Each child was given the test individually. He was shown the test film and then given 25 minutes to ask questions to gather the data he needed and to construct his explanatory system. We tape-recorded these individual inquiry sessions and used the tape as the basis of our analysis of each child's inquiry behavior.

While we actually identified some 12 question types that could be clearly differentiated, it is more meaningful to point out the three major categories of questions. One of these was *verification*. This category included all questions that are attempts to identify and analyze the parameters of the problem episode; questions about the names of objects, the materials they were made out of, the conditions of objects such as temperature, pressure, shape, size; the events of the episode, and the properties of objects in the episode.

The second major question type was what we call the *implication* question. These questions are probes used to test out ideas of causal relationships. They go beyond the verification of what happened into the realm of why things happen. Implication questions have two important subdivisions. Some questions in this category are attempts to verify relationships between variables in a direct, abstract way. This question type is called "abstract-conceptual." An example of this would be: "Does the bending of the blade have anything to do with the heat?" The question is, in effect, a direct request for the verification of an idea. Abstract-conceptual questions are requests for judgments about causation and therefore short-circuit the process of inquiry. Because the questioner obtains a direct evaluation of his hypothesis he avoids the necessity of testing the hypothesis experimentally, of gathering data and making his own inferences.

The second type of implication question is called "concrete-inferential." These questions are more like experiments. An example would be: "If we made the flame hotter, would the blade bend further?" In this case the child is manipulating a variable and simply asking if a particular outcome would be the result of his manipulation. But he makes his own inference as to causality from the data he obtains.

Our attempt in Inquiry Training was to increase the amount of verification and the amount of experimentation and to decrease the abstract-conceptual "brain-picking" kind of questioning.

In our analysis of the Questest protocols for the experimental and the control groups, we found first of all that in every case the inquiry-trained groups asked significantly more questions than the controls. It was necessary therefore to control for fluency in comparing the groups in terms of the frequencies of the major question types. We found that where fluency was high the inquiry-trained groups asked significantly more verification questions than the controls and significantly less abstract-conceptual implication questions than the controls. There was no noticeable difference between the two groups in the use of experimentation.

With respect to conceptual growth, our finding was that in most cases conceptual growth through the inquiry approach was about the same as the growth attained under the more traditional didactic methods. We did have two groups, however, in which the inquiry-trained children had significantly higher scores on the concept test than the control children.

Of course, the real test of Inquiry Training would be the degree to which a child is able to transfer his inquiry skills to problems in other content areas. If inquiry is a mode of behavior and can be developed and strengthened through practice and through the deliberate shaping of strategies and techniques, then this behavior should be applicable in a wide range of problem situations.

We are now engaged in an investigation to test the transfer effects of Inquiry Training. New problem films are now being developed in economics and biology. Sometime next year we will give a group of sixth grade children Inquiry Training using our physics films and then determine how effective they are in solving economics and biology problems through the inquiry approach.

Implications for Curriculum

We do not see the specific techniques and methodology of Inquiry Training as we have used it thus far as the significant outcome of our work. We have been far more concerned with the theoretical implications of our findings. What has impressed us most in our observation of the inquiry process is that the autonomy of the learner has enormous importance for both motivation and conceptual growth. Take away from the child the element of choice in the learning process and you destroy one of the most potent forces for keeping the child involved in learning and for giving him an opportunity to influence the course of his own learning. Self-direction in learning is not a case of the blind leading the blind because the learner is in a position to know the nature and the location of his conceptual gaps. He is sensitive to his own informational needs. If he is not given an opportunity to modify and at least to some extent to direct his own data intake, his learning experiences may well miss the mark by a wide margin.

We have just begun to explore the possibilities of introducing the inquiry approach and Inquiry Training into the curriculum. This approach should not be brought in as a thing apart from "regular subjects," as a "gimmick" or special shot in the arm. Possibly what is needed is an inquiry-centered curriculum in which the children would find themselves launched into areas of study by first being confronted by concrete problem-focused episodes for which they would attempt to build explanatory systems. Part of their data gathering might well be in the question-asking mode and certainly along the way time would have to be spent in building inquiry skills through critiques and other such procedures. Yet there would also be room for helping the children enlarge their conceptual systems through more teacher-directed means. At times the teacher might work with groups in developing new conceptual models or in identifying variables that might be useful for analysis of the problem episode. Of course, the children would still be using the library and other materials, but always in relation to a particular problem of inquiry. Learning would always be in connection with moving from concrete events toward the construction of an explanatory model. Yet neither the analysis of the concrete events nor the particular models constructed to explain them would be the most important outcome of these inquiries. There would be three and possibly more by-products that would have far greater significance.

First there would be the development and strengthening of the inquiry process itself. Since learning would always be couched within the inquiry framework, the children would become more autonomous learners and their motivation in the process of learning would be greater. The second by-product would be the self-image that would develop in the children as a result of a greater autonomy in learning. The children would emerge with a sense of intellectual potency and a faith in the regularity of the universe and a greater skepticism toward any explanatory system as a final and ultimate truth. They would learn to question and test and to see themselves as able to move from data to theory under their own power. This should boost their self-confidence for making further inquiries and for resisting efforts by others to program them into accepting a predetermined conclusion.

A third consequence of such a curriculum would be the development of a greater depth of understanding of principles and concepts within the disciplines of study relevant to the problems posed for inquiry. The child who inquires into the bimetallic strip can never emerge with a complete explanation of the events observed, but he can come to grips with such fundamental physical principles as conduction, the theory of molecular structure, the relationship between volume and temperature in matter, the principles governing stress and strain in metals. In Bruner's terms he will penetrate the structures of the disciplines concerned and become rather intimately involved with some segments of those structures.

Finally, the inquiry-centered curriculum would break away from the rhetoric of conclusions which now dominates so much of the curriculum and would put the process and products of scientific inquiry back into their proper relationship.

References

R. Alpert. *The Shaping of Motives in Education.* Speech prepared for the Fifth ASCD Curriculum Research Institute, 1960.

M. Beberman. *An Emerging Program of Secondary School Mathematics.* Cambridge: Harvard University Press, 1958.

J. S. Bruner *et al. A Study of Thinking.* New York: John Wiley & Sons, 1958.

J. S. Bruner. "The Act of Discovery." *Harvard Educational Review* 31: 21-32; 1961.

E. Erikson. *Childhood and Society.* New York: W. W. Norton & Company, Inc., 1950.

L. Festinger. *A Theory of Cognitive Dissonance.* Evanston, Illinois: Row, Peterson & Company, 1957.

J. W. Getzels and P. W. Jackson. *Creativity and Intelligence*. New York: John Wiley & Sons, 1962.

J. P. Guilford *et al.* "A Factor-analytic Study of Creative Thinking." *Reports from the Psychology Laboratory*. Los Angeles: University of Southern California Press, 1952.

Gertrude Hendrix. "Learning by Discovery." *Mathematics Teacher* 54: 290-99; 1961.

J. McV. Hunt. *Piaget's Observations as a Source of Hypotheses Concerning Motivation*. Paper read at the Annual Meeting, American Psychological Association, 1962.

Bärbel Inhelder and J. Piaget. *The Growth of Logical Thinking from Childhood to Adolescence*. New York: Basic Books, 1958.

J. Kagan, H. Moss and I. Sigel. *The Psychological Significance of Styles of Conceptualization*. A paper read at a Conference on Basic Cognitive Processes sponsored by the Social Science Research Council, 1961.

D. MacKinnon. "Fostering Creativity in Students of Engineering." *Journal of Engineering Education* 52: 129-42; 1961.

J. Piaget and Bärbel Inhelder. *Le Développement des Quantités chez L'Enfant*. Dalachaux et Niestle, 1941.

J. R. Suchman. "Inquiry Training in the Elementary School." *Science Teacher* 27 (7): 42-47; 1960.

J. R. Suchman. "Inquiry Training: Building Skills for Autonomous Discovery." *Merrill-Palmer Quarterly* 7: 147-69; 1961.

J. R. Suchman. *The Elementary School Training Program in Scientific Inquiry*. Illinois Studies in Inquiry Training. Urbana: University of Illinois, 1962. (Mimeographed.)

E. P. Torrance. *Guiding Creative Talent*. Englewood Cliffs, New Jersey: Prentice Hall Incorporated, 1962.

R. W. White. "Motivation Reconsidered: The Concept of Competence." *Psychological Review* 66: 297-333; 1959.

One Physicist
Looks at Science Education

Robert Karplus

IN SPITE of my specialized background, my interests in science teaching are at the level of general education. For this reason I refer to "science education" and not to "physics education" or "chemistry education." Most of the students I have in mind will not become scientists. Though they cannot devote much time and effort to education in science, all citizens seriously need to have some understanding of scientific attitudes, procedures and concepts. Unfortunately, the adult population at present seems to have only a very poor understanding of these. Since science will continue to play a significant role in every individual's life, it is important that educational practices be adopted to prepare students more effectively to meet the challenges that will face them.

I should define the role I see in science curriculum improvement for scientists like myself. Until very recently, we have not participated in educational activities. It is therefore to be expected that we cannot understand all aspects of education. What we can do is to suggest ways of looking at natural phenomena that the scientist has found productive. By developing illustrative experiments and presenting these to the student with questions and suggestions, we can seek to lead him to observe the significant properties of the experimental system. How successful we are is really not a question we can answer by ourselves. That is a question to be answered by the educational community as a whole.

In this article, I shall describe some characteristics of natural

NOTE: The experiments described in this article were carried out by the author at the Berkwood School, Berkeley, California, through the cooperation of the Director, Betty Halpern. Financial support for the project was provided by the National Science Foundation, Washington, D. C.

phenomena that seem to be especially significant for general education. They illustrate fundamental ways in which the scientific point of view differs from and goes beyond the natural logic or common sense point of view that individuals in our culture develop as they grow up (1, 2). In the first two sections, I review how my experimental work led me to recognize the nature of this gap and why I believe that attempts to bridge it must start during the elementary school years. Following this background material, I briefly point out that observation and interpretation play comparable roles in the development of science. The science curriculum, which has to pay attention to both these aspects, is described in quite general terms in the next section; just how they fit together is a most interesting question. Two further sections give a survey of the teaching program that the Science Curriculum Improvement Study is developing under my direction. First there is a discussion of the major science concepts that underlie the scientific point of view. There follows an outline of a few lessons that have been used in experimental teaching programs to communicate to primary school pupils an understanding of some of the concepts and their interrelation. In the conclusion, finally, I sketch the relation of this program to the science curriculum in the subsequent school years.

Beginning the Study

In July 1959, with financial support from the National Science Foundation, a group of scientists and educators at the University of California in Berkeley began a study for curriculum improvement in elementary school science. Inevitably, the first year of operation furnished particularly an opportunity for learning. The results have been described in other articles in some detail (3, 4, 5, 6). Here I shall review only the most significant findings.

How was the study used as a learning experience for the participants? One way would have been to review the very extensive research literature in science education, the available textbooks, the courses of study, and the work of science teachers. This was not done. Instead I undertook to write two teachers' manuals concurrently with doing some experimental teaching of the same two topics [1] (7, 8). The reason why this second procedure had to be chosen was clear. Without concrete experience in teaching and writing, a critical review of the literature was impossible; in fact, without this experience the educational literature was largely meaningless.

[1] The topics were chosen because they were scientifically important, because I had some ideas about teaching them, and because they were not a part of the usual elementary science program. They dealt with graph drawing and with the laws of motion.

Given my knowledge and experience at the time, I really had to learn "from the ground up" or I could only imitate without understanding or judgment what had been done before. One might say I had to become "educationally literate" just as I should like the school children to become scientifically literate. And it is my conviction that the only basis for literacy in a radically new field is concrete experience by the learner, no matter what his age or level of sophistication may be.

Since I have a particular interest in physics, I shall describe here what I learned from the teaching experience with the unit on force and the laws of motion. The idea of force was introduced through the use of examples such as a child pushing on the desk with his hand or pulling a wagon. The idea was later applied to the changes in motion that result when a force acts on an object. Even though the children participated in the experiments with enthusiasm, they and the teachers had serious difficulty grasping the concepts.

Further exploratory work with children suggested that two crucial ideas were misunderstood. The first of these can be illustrated by the examples that were used to introduce force. The pupils identified the exertion of force with the activity of their muscles. From the common sense point of view, this is quite reasonable. Scientifically, however, it is incorrect. The force exerted by the hand on the desk, for instance, must be grasped in terms of only these two objects, the hand and the desk, which affect each other. When this separation is not made, and when force is associated with a single object (the muscle) rather than with the interaction of two objects, the force concept loses its meaning.

The second difficulty arose with the concept of motion. Most individuals are accustomed to consider motion as an activity (*i.e.*, locomotion) and perceive it in relation to the immediate surroundings of the object. For instance, can a box move? Most people will say no, not by itself. They do not separate the motion from whatever causes the motion. Even aside from this question, one may ask whether the box in a moving truck is moving or is staying in the same place. The driver will glance at it occasionally to make sure that it has stayed in the same place on the truck. The customer, on the other hand, is pleased that the box has not remained in the same place, that it is now near his home and no longer in the warehouse.

From these remarks, it appears that the conceptual structure of science is different from the conceptual structure of common sense. A layman is not accustomed to perceive phenomena in the same way as a scientist. Even a scientist is likely to have two levels of perception, the scientific one and the "ordinary" one. One general way in which the difference manifests itself is that the common sense concern is largely with purpose and motivation, while the scientist is concerned with causes in a more mechanistic way. Thus the two statements, "I started the car because I wanted to drive to work," and "The starting motor turned because the circuit to the battery was closed," are both correct, but are also very different. The first one is much more significant in human terms, the second one has objective reliability. The science teacher has to recognize the difference and build his program on this awareness.

Why Elementary School Science?

Given that science is a vital part of the general education of every citizen, there are strong reasons why science teaching should begin in the elementary school and not be postponed to later years. In the age range from six to fourteen years the child's thinking undergoes a gradual transition from concrete to abstract. At the beginning of this period the child is achieving mastery of his muscles and gaining the ability to carry out physical manipulations; in his thinking he is dependent on direct experience. At the end of the transition the child is achieving a degree of mastery of mind; he is able to focus his thoughts consciously and to manipulate abstract relationships without constant reference to specific examples (9, 10, 11, 12).

There is a temptation to postpone science instruction until the youngsters have reached the intellectual maturity of the middle teens. Educational efforts at this stage, however, reach only the fraction of the student body which is favorably disposed toward science because of earlier favorable experience at home or at school. For the others, many of whom form a strong distaste for science, it is too late.

What do these observations have to do with science teaching? Just this. The present content of science consists of concepts and relationships that mankind has abstracted from the observation of natural phenomena over the centuries. This content represents the outcome of a long, slow process. During the elementary school years, boys and girls are engaged in precisely this kind of abstracting process with respect to their own natural environment. The function of education is to guide children's development by providing them with particularly informative and suggestive experiences as a base for their abstractions. At the same time, children must be provided with a conceptual framework that permits them to perceive the phenomena in a meaningful way and to integrate their inferences into generalizations of lasting value.

I should like to stress that I consider the conceptual framework to be an essential part of science, a part that can be developed in a properly guided substantive study of material phenomena. The development that takes place in the absence of such instruction is haphazard and leads to many invalid generalizations that are serious obstacles to later learning. The superstitions and fears regarding natural phenomena in primitive societies and even among adults in our own advanced culture illustrate this point.

The elementary school science program has been described in terms similar to these by many educators who have concerned themselves with the general features that science courses should have (13, 14, 15). Nevertheless, there is general agreement that current teaching practices do not entirely meet the pupils' needs. One great weakness seems to be a heavy reliance on textbooks and other secondary materials as sources of information. These sources for science learning are quite impotent compared to the direct experiences that nourish the pupils' intellectual development of "common sense" rationality. Instead of guiding this development, therefore, the science course creates a second, separate, and relatively abstract structure that is not much used outside the school situation and which eventually atrophies or even results in a resentment against science.

It is most important that each student learn to find his own answers, even if they differ from everyone else's. By repeating experiments and comparing notes, the class as a whole can achieve a good understanding of the phenomenon under study. When all pupils get the same result, little is learned. When the results fluctuate around a mean, appreciation is created for the variability of the conclusion subject to certain errors. When the results vary violently, the experiment was poorly designed. Nevertheless, each pupil should feel strongly about the integrity of his own observations; without this attitude, no science is possible.

What I have written must not be interpreted to mean that a pupil can learn only what he observes himself. The world is too complicated to permit a single individual to learn all he should in one lifetime. It does mean, however, that the early years of school should provide a sufficiently diversified program based heavily on concrete experiences. The difficult part, which is often overlooked, is that the concrete experiences must be presented in a context that helps to build a conceptual framework (16). Then, and only then, will the early learning form a base for the assimilation of experiences that come later, experiences that may involve direct observation or the report of observations made by others.

In other words, to be able to use information obtained by others, the individual must have a conceptual structure and a means of communication that enable him to interpret the information as though he had obtained it himself. We shall call this functional understanding of science concepts "scientific literacy." It is the principal objective of the elementary school science program.

The Nature and Structure of Science

I have pointed out the important role that observation plays in science, a role which it should also play in science teaching. It may appear, therefore, that the starting point of a scientific endeavor is an actual observation. From a number of similar observations the scientist formulates a hypothesis about the behavior of a class of objects in the kind of situation he has studied. He then continues to make observations in further situations to which he expects his hypothesis to apply. If the behavior turns out always to be consistent with his expectation, the hypothesis is confirmed and thereafter may be called a law of nature. If the behavior turns out to be contrary to his expectation, the hypothesis in its original form must be abandoned.

For example, let us consider a piece of iron which expands when it is heated. After additional observations (the expansion of brass, wood, alcohol, and air on heating) we are ready to formulate a hypothesis: all substances expand when heated at constant pressure. We now continue to experiment. Sooner or later we study the expansion of water and find that it contracts when heated from 32 to 40°F. That's the end of the hypothesis as stated. Can we modify it successfully? The "hypothesis of universal thermal expansion" could be changed to "all gases expand when heated at constant pressure." In this form it could be called a law of nature.

As a second example, let us consider a ball released without support which falls to the ground. After additional observations (the dropping to the ground of pieces of wood, of a feather, and of a glass bowl), we are again ready to formulate a hypothesis: all objects fall to the ground when released without support. We now continue to experiment. Eventually, we release a helium-filled balloon and find that it does not drop; instead it rises. That is the end of this hypothesis. Can we modify it successfully? The "hypothesis of universal gravity" could be changed to "all objects fall to the ground when released without support in a vacuum." It is still sensible only near the earth or another large heavenly body. In space, far from the earth, "falling to the ground" is meaningless because there is no "ground."

We have so far overlooked two elements in the forming of hypotheses. One is the judgment as to what constitutes "similar" observations. In our example, for instance, it is possible to consider the balloon so different from the other objects that its behavior is not considered relevant to the "hypothesis of universal gravity." Also there is the question of whether the heavenly bodies, the moon, for instance, are objects to which the hypothesis is to apply. The second is the judgment as to what aspects of the observations are to be compared. Again in our example, are we concerned that the bodies move when they are released, or that they ultimately come to rest? Before an ordinary scientific study can take place, these two types of questions have to be answered.

Usually the answers are implicitly assumed and agreed upon by the members of the scientific community and constitute what we may call the "scientific point of view." One element of this point of view is the assumption that natural phenomena are reproducible: that under a given set of conditions the same behavior will ensue. Other elements have to do with the form of an acceptable explanation of a phenomenon. Occasionally, however, new observations create serious difficulties in understanding when they are considered from the current point of view. Then there is the need for bold and imaginative thinking to develop a new point of view that shows more promise of being able to deal successfully with the known phenomena. Eventually this may become the accepted "scientific point of view" (17).

I should now correct the statement I made at the beginning of this section: more accurately, the starting point of a scientific endeavor is an actual observation interpreted in the light of the "scientific point of view." Of course, the "scientific point of view" is not given in advance of all observation. It represents a synthesis of past experience. But at any given moment, it defines a context for the interpretation of any specific observation (18).

I have noted that the scientist abstracts a common quality from similar situations (the concept of expansion in the one example). A hypothesis is a statement about such an abstraction. Now he can build further. Once a number of similar hypotheses have been established, he can seek to abstract a common quality from them, and then conjecture a hypothesis about this more abstract concept. The atomic and molecular structure of matter is such a higher order abstraction that has been inferred from many laws of the behavior of gases, liquids, and solids. In this way, a highly abstract conceptual structure, quite remote from specific observations, can be constructed. With the help of such a structure, and with the requirement that it not contradict itself, the theoretical scientists can draw conclusions in one area of applications from observations in a second area that appears to be quite remote from the first. In such a structure it is also possible to carry out so-called indirect measurements, in which direct observations are combined with hypotheses to yield more information.

The elaborate structure should not obscure the fact that at the base of science lies the observation interpreted from a particular point of view. Science is never complete; there are always some unanswered questions, some unexpected phenomena. These may eventually be resolved within the accepted structure of science or they may force a revision of the fundamental point of view from which the phenomenon was interpreted. Progress in science comes from the discovery of new phenomena and from the invention of novel interpretations that illuminate in a new way the new and the well-known phenomena (17). Scientific truth is therefore not absolute and permanent; rather it is in accordance with the facts as currently known (18). Without this qualification, the statement that scientists seek the truth is misleading. It is better to say that scientists seek understanding.

The Science Curriculum

I turn now to consider the implication of the preceding remarks for the science curriculum. The teaching objective is to give the students sufficient knowledge and experience so they will be able to have some understanding of scientific work being carried out by others even though they themselves do not become scientists. This quality I have called scientific literacy.

The introduction of "laboratory blocks" into high school physics, chemistry, and biology courses is a large step in this direction (19). Only by carrying out investigations himself can the student become acquainted with the experience of wrestling with a scientific problem. To carry out such an investigation, however, the student has to have an adequate background so he can sense the existence of a scientific problem and can construct a tentative approach to its solution. This means he must be able to look at the problem situation from the "scientific point of view."

Many persons believe that the real usefulness of these ambitious high school programs will become apparent only when the previous education of the student prepares him appropriately (20, 21). One measure of the effectiveness of the elementary school and junior high school science programs will be the performance of the students in high school. In all likelihood, therefore, the high school courses will have to be revised once the possibilities of elementary school science have been explored. At present, the difficulties that students experience at the high school level can focus the attention of the curriculum designer on crucial areas to which he must pay special attention.

These crucial areas are basic to what I have called the "scientific point of view." They present difficulties to the students because of their divergence from the common notions about the natural environment that everyone takes for granted and that are seldom questioned. Benjamin Lee Whorf has observed (22):

. . . if a rule has absolutely no exceptions, it is not recognized as a rule or as anything else; it is then part of the background of experience of which we tend to remain unconscious. Never having experienced anything in contrast to it, we cannot isolate it and formulate it as a rule until we so enlarge our experience and expand our base of reference that we encounter an interruption of its regularity. The situation is somewhat analogous to that of not missing the water till the well runs dry, or not realizing that we need air till we are choking.

Since the scientific point of view is based on more diversified experience than that of one individual, many rules are established that seem tautologous when applied to the restricted range of phenomena that are easily accessible. Suppose, for example, the teacher holds a block, releases it, and it drops. Why did it drop? Most pupils will say, "Because you let go." This answer is the only sensible one for terrestrial pupils. Gravitation is part of the background against which they view experience. Deviation from the normal behavior, e.g., the block's not falling, is noted and ascribed to a cause—the hand holds the block. When the cause ceases to act, normal behavior is resumed. Only by comparing terrestrial with astronomical observations does it make sense to speak of gravity.

In order to reach the objective of scientific literacy, therefore, the science curriculum has to provide the pupils with experiences that are different from their usual ones. The difference may have to do with the substances that are manipulated. These substances can be hard or soft, elastic or inelastic, more dense or less dense, brittle or ductile, chemically active or inert. For instance, most objects commonly used have a specific gravity between 0.8 and 3. Polystyrene foam pieces and cast iron skillets, whose density falls outside this range, create quite an impression because their qualities are uncommon.

Another type of experience is based on instruments or devices that may extend the range of the senses. Magnifying glasses, microscopes and telescopes permit visual observation and comparisons that are out of the ordinary. Thermometers, spring scales, voltameters, graduated cylinders, and stroboscopes make possible the discovery of quantitative equivalences.

A third kind of experience has to do with unusual environmental conditions. The sensation of apparent weightlessness in an orbiting satellite would obviously be very interesting, but will be outside the reach of elementary school pupils for some time to come. An express elevator with sudden starts and stops is the closest most of us will come to "weightlessness." A rotating platform such as a merry-go-round is a "floor" on which the laws of nature are different from the customary ones. A completely dark space and space illuminated with light of only one color lead to a re-examination of the role of light.

A fourth kind of experience, finally, is based on the observation of living organisms. Many organisms are not commonly available or cannot usually be observed under controlled conditions. Yet some exhibit characteristic behavior patterns in an extreme form that calls attention to similar behavior in other organisms in which it is too subtle to be noticed easily. That animals exhibit what is called "behavior" is already a very significant learning, for example.

A most interesting pedagogical question concerns the manner in which these experiences should be incorporated into the teaching program. I hope it is clear that the experiences should be direct ones for the children, not told by the teacher or read in a book. To see photographs taken through a microscope, to have someone tell about feeling a piece of lead, are completely inadequate substitutes for looking or feeling for oneself. There is, however, the question of how much guidance the teacher or the book should provide for the children as they manipulate and observe and how much discussion and review should follow the experience. How much verbalization should take place?

It is my belief that there should be substantial guidance and discussion (10, 23). There should be an effort to relate the unusual experience to the more usual experience of which it represents an extreme case. In this way, the abstract concepts that are at the basis of the scientific point of view are built up. As the children make further observations, they will look at them more scientifically. The abstractions will form a link between their earlier experience and later experience, so that the children can bring to bear their knowledge in a systematic way. Perhaps the gulf between scientific thinking and common sense thinking can be reduced!

Each lesson in the science program may fulfill one or both of these functions: to provide a new experience and to establish or reinforce an abstract concept. Connections among different lessons are created by use of the same phenomenon to illustrate different concepts and the use of the same concept to interpret different phenomena. The conceptual structure creates a context for the new experience that enables it to be assimilated rationally in relation to other experiences. One might say that the structure provides discipline for mental organization.

Major Science Concepts

When a scientist considers a phenomenon, his first concern is for the real or physical objects that appear to participate. He may not recognize or even detect all of them immediately, but he makes a tentative inventory. This inventory of objects he calls the "system" that he will use to study the phenomenon. As his understanding advances, he may find that his original identification did not emphasize the objects which later emerge as significant. He then defines a new system that promises to be more useful and abandons the original selection.

This fact of being conscious of the participating material objects is important, because the scientist is likely to have encountered the objects before, even if they were never grouped in the same way. By making the identification, he can relate the new observations to his previous experience with the same or with similar objects. It is not an easy matter to determine which objects participate in a phenomenon. Some may be present but may not be involved. In spite of this difficulty, attention to the material realities is more conducive to progress in understanding than a focus on more personal impressions that the phenomenon creates in the observer.

One of the first tasks of the science program, therefore, is to reinforce the children's growing awareness of material objects (24) and of their properties and to check their own animistic interpretations. The task is helped by using the word "object" and by relating objects to other objects instead of relating each object to a purposeful use by the child. There are many nursery school and kindergarten activities which involve the comparison and sorting of collections of objects according to various properties such as shape, size, color and composition. Eventually each object should be seen as a member of many overlapping classes; a tennis ball, for example, is a round object, a white object, a soft object, a fuzzy object, etc. After all, it is through a common class membership that new objects are related to ones with which the individual is familiar. According to Vygotsky (23), verbal labels are important in the establishment of class concepts. Hence attention by the school to this aspect of organizing experiences may substantially help the children, who have extensive nonverbal experience with many objects outside school.

Working with the gross properties of single objects does not involve the study of any natural phenomena at this educational level.[2] The children's attention is therefore now directed at pairs of objects, where the two objects are doing something to each other. The clay sticks to the wall, the scissors cut the paper, the bat hits the ball, are all examples with which the children have experience. The general scientific concept that corresponds to this relationship of two objects affecting or influencing each other is the *concept of interaction*. It includes the cases mentioned, but also the case of the sun and the earth, the earth and the moon, a magnet and a nail, a magnet and a current-carrying wire, chemical processes, two atoms colliding, and so on.

Whenever a scientist tries to explain a phenomenon, he reduces it to the mutual influence or interaction of the participating physical objects. He may continue his quest and seek to explain the interaction in terms of a structure for each of the objects which is itself made out

---

[2] At a later stage some interesting science problems will revolve around the perceptual mechanism for distinguishing these properties.

of smaller objects; and the smaller objects are in turn capable of interactions. So the explanation goes on until the supposed fundamental objects or particles and the supposed fundamental interactions are reached. For them there is no further explanation at present. There is only a justification—they serve to explain the chain of phenomena that was studied.

One of the most exciting fields of current research has to do with the genetic code—how characteristics of one living cell are passed along to the daughter cells. Once this was explained in terms of the influence of the cell nucleus on the protoplasm. Later it was found that the nucleus contained chromosomes, and that the chromosomes interacted with the protoplasm. The next step involved genes, and the next step DNA molecules interacting with the protoplasm molecules. Now the structure of DNA is being determined, so that the fundamental interaction is currently the one between the molecular fragments of DNA and protein molecules of the protoplasm. Eventually, biophysicists will find an explanation in terms of interactions between specific atoms or even between certain electrons in the atoms.

The fundamental physical interactions, which are at present unexplained, are the gravitational interactions, the electromagnetic interactions, the nuclear interactions, and interactions of radioactivity. It appears that all specific events can be explained in terms of these interactions. Whether they, in turn, will some day be explained by still more fundamental interactions is not known. How all characteristics of life can be explained is also not known.

One revolutionary trend was introduced by Einstein some fifty years ago with the general theory of relativity. In this theory, the gravitational interaction does not remain fundamental, but is explained in terms of the structure of space itself. The structure of space is more fundamental and is unexplained. Whether other interactions can also be treated in this way is still an open question.

One of the difficulties in teaching the interaction concept is that an interaction cannot be associated with a single object, but has to do with a relationship between two or more objects. To help overcome this problem, it is convenient to group together the interacting objects in what is called a "system." I have used this word before to refer to the grouping of objects that participate in a phenomenon. Now the notion of "participating" has been made more precise; those objects participate which are capable of interacting with the others. One can also see how the interaction concept is a background for the understanding of force. The force exerted by object A on object B is that aspect of their mutual interaction which tends to change the velocity of object B.

For practical reasons, it is usually desirable to disregard some apparently insignificant interactions and to idealize others. If this were not done, the system would always consist of the whole universe, since actually all objects interact with all others directly or indirectly. Yet individual distant stars merely produce a negligible effect on all terrestrial objects (except on the eye at the end of the telescope observing that star). Likewise, the hand holding the test tube does not affect the dissolving of the crystals in the water in the test tube (unless it raises the temperature a little bit or shakes the test tube). In fact, the test tube itself is not important for the solution process (unless it is somewhat soluble too).

The motivation for the choice of a physical system is derived from a desire to study interactions. One will choose the system in such a way that the most important interactions occur between the objects in the system, and that the interactions between objects in the system and objects outside are of less concern. In the game of tug-of-war (two boys and a rope), the boys interact not only with the rope, but also with the floor. This interaction, which depends on the boys' shoes and can be decisive, would suggest that a more useful system might include the two boys, the rope, and the floor. The presence of interactions therefore supplies a criterion that can help in the definition of useful systems.

All these provisos make the grouping of objects into a system a quite sophisticated task. For the school children, who are just beginning to get acquainted with all the interactions, both important and unimportant, the choice of system is a matter of trial and learning. The initial choice of objects in the system should be kept quite open; the only mistake that can be made in defining a system is to include processes or interactions such as "stretching" or "spinning" that are not material objects. It is possible, however, to be inconsistent in using the system concept. That would be the case if one were to treat a particular object as being sometimes a component of the system and sometimes, in the same discussion, as being outside the system. The instructor should make clear that the choice of system is free, but that once a system is chosen, the system has to be used consistently until it is abandoned.

When the system is defined, the children point out interactions between objects in the system, and between objects in the system and objects in the environment. Now the class as a whole may decide that one of the latter interactions is very important. Then the pupils will choose a new system, with one of the objects of the old environment included in the new system. Similarly, an object may have been included at first even though it turns out not to interact appreciably; in the redefinition of the system, this object is left out. If the children are not able to decide the relative importance of the various interactions, then the task of analyzing the phenomenon was too complicated and a simpler situation should be chosen. In my work with second and third graders, I have dealt with systems containing up to four or five distinct objects.

Besides furnishing a context for the discussion and evaluation of interactions, the system has an important conservation property. Throughout a phenomenon, one can keep track of what passes from the system to the environment and what enters the system from the environment. One can therefore set up bookkeeping to compare the initial and final states. This bookkeeping will be simple because the definition of the system minimizes or controls the exchanges of matter and energy with the environment. One special and most interesting case is the isolated system: here there are no interactions at all with the environment.

Let me now restate the relationship of system, object, and interaction in a way that emphasizes how each derives meaning from the others. The specific system is determined by the significance a person attaches to each component object in relation to the other objects present. Once a child has decided what interests him, he can describe or define the physical system that he wishes to use at that time. He can then communicate the fact that he has made his choice by stating what system he has selected. Different children may choose different systems for thinking about a particular experiment. When there is a discussion, however, the entire class must agree on the system the class will use; otherwise the discussion will lead to confusion. In other words, the choice of a system is merely a conscious way to define what group of objects one is talking or thinking about.

Now, what is an object? It is a component of a system, of course. Yet there are often many ways in which a system can sensibly be divided into components. Let a flashlight be the system, for instance. Then the objects in this system could be the one flashlight, or the two dry cells and the case, or the dry cells, the metal shell, the bulb, and the glass cover, or all the molecules, or all the atoms, or all the electrons and protons and neutrons. No one of these is more correct than the others. Each is a useful way of thinking about the flashlight. The child in the dark would choose the first way, the salesclerk in the store would choose the second, the inquiring boy would choose the third, the chemist would choose one of the last three.

The meaning of the terms, "system" and "object," therefore, is determined by the interest of the scientist. The system is the totality of what is interesting, the objects are the units whose finer structure is currently uninteresting. The solar system, which contains the sun and planets as objects, may itself be treated as an object in the study of the entire galaxy, and an individual galaxy may be treated as an object when the universe is the system. Similarly, an atom can be an object in a crystal, but an atom can also be a system whose components are electrons and nucleus. Any collection of objects may be a system. It is a system, however, only after someone has made the decision to select it.

When a system is defined and the objects are identified, one must ask what the objects are doing to each other, how they are interacting. Thus, in the system of floor and table, the floor holds up the table; in the system of sun and flower, the sun shines on the flower; in a tug-of-war game (two boys and a rope), each boy pulls on the rope. One can also distinguish between direct interactions, where the objects are in contact, and distant interactions (e.g., sun and flower) where they are not in contact. Of course, the word "contact" is not defined, but it does have a quite clear intuitive meaning. Only later, when the atomic structure of matter is considered, will the pupils be forced to reconsider the notion of physical contact between two objects.

In addition to studying what objects in a system can do to each other, it is important to study what they are doing, that is, how they are moving. In order to help separate the descriptive "How" from the causal "How?", I invented an artificial observer. The observer notices where every object in the system is at all times, but he does not wonder why anything happens. He is, therefore, different from children. Furthermore he is completely egocentric in his descriptions; he observes the position of everything relative to himself. Thus an observer on the sun describes the earth as orbiting about the sun and revolving on its axis. An observer fixed on the earth describes the sun and moon as revolving about the earth. An observer fixed on the moon describes the earth as fairly stationary and observes the sun rising and setting once every four weeks. All three observers are describing the same phenomenon, each from his own egocentric point of view. The important idea behind this concept of observer is that it is possible and valuable to consider descriptions from several points of view.

The four major concepts—objects, systems, the observer, and interactions—deal with the material content of the universe, with its behavior, and with man's interpretation of this behavior. These concepts in turn lead to others; a schematic outline is indicated in the accompanying chart.[3] Some additional words here will indicate what I believe about the upper entries in the chart. Several of the other entries are discussed in the next section. All observations and descriptions are based on comparisons. If one compares different systems at the same time, one speaks of similarities and differences with regard to various properties of the system. If one compares the same system at different times, one speaks of conservation and change. The interaction concept is used to account for specific

[3] See Chart 1.

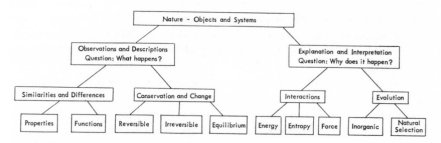

changes in a single system. The concept of evolution is used to account for the cumulative effect of many changes over such a long period of time that it is not useful to speak of the identity of a single system throughout the process. Interaction and evolution are the fundamental explanatory concepts in the current scientific point of view.

Sample Teaching Experiences

During the past four years I have been trying to determine whether the ideas outlined in the previous section can be implemented in elementary school classrooms. Here are the descriptions of a few lessons that have been found effective in some first and second grades.

Interaction: The school children already have an interaction concept in the sense of one object doing something to another. They use many words such as pull, push, cut, sweep, scrape, shine on, and stick together, to describe the interaction in individual cases. Their concept, however, is not well differentiated from the concepts of action or behavior, which also are defined by verbs. One important generalization the children have to recognize is that an interaction involves at least two objects. Thus "I am running" describes an activity or behavior, while "my shoe scrapes the floor" describes an interaction. A focus on the specific objects interacting rather than a focus on the whole situation helps to define the concept because it reduces the likelihood of interfering thoughts. For example, the statement, "I scrape the floor" instead of "my shoe scrapes the floor," conveys the idea of an activity as well as of an interaction.

In the first lesson the pupils described what various objects in the class were doing to each other. They also made pictures to illustrate "cut," "shine on," "pull," "push," etc., by drawing appropriate objects (*e.g.*, scissors and paper, sun and flower) in a more or less appropriate relationship. In the second lesson the pictures were reviewed and displayed on the bulletin board under the heading, "Objects Interact." The word "interact" was introduced as a generalization of all the specific verbs they had illustrated. In the third lesson each child did experiments with some objects selected from a box provided by the teacher. The objects included paper, pencils, scissors, candy, water, thumbtacks, paper clips, string, magnets, batteries, light bulbs, and wires. After the experiment, each child described how the objects had behaved and which ones had interacted.

These lessons, of course, only established a base for the development of the interaction concept. They made it possible for the pupils to discover other examples of interactions. For instance, the coat and the coat hanger may interact, the thumbtack and the water interact, the candy and the tongue interact, the flower roots and the soil interact, and so on. Each time a new situation is interpreted by means of the interaction concept, the concept is enriched. By directing the children's attention to the interaction concept, the teacher created for them a new way of looking at and interpreting their environment (25).

Equilibrium: The elementary school pupils have a strongly developed sense of distinction between activity and quiescence. I pointed out several times how this sense of activity interfered with teaching attempts that did not take this distinction into account. The scientist makes a similar distinction: He describes some systems as being at equilibrium and some systems as being not at equilibrium. The lesson on equilibrium was intended to give the children a new way of interpreting their recognition of activity and change.

The pupils were allowed to examine a display of many systems that included a burning candle, a spring, an ice cube in water, sugar crystals in water, a stone in water, mechanical turtles, several piles of blocks, and a flashlight that was turned on. The toy turtle was wound up and permitted to walk on the table. At first the children were asked to define systems for the many experiments in progress. After all examples had been mentioned, the class discussed the fact that not all systems were remaining the same. In some, the arrangement of the component objects was changing: the candle was burning up, the ice cube was melting, the sugar was dissolving, etc. In others, like the rock in the water, the piled up blocks and the spring, nothing was happening. Now the teacher introduced a new term: the static systems were said to be at equilibrium, while the ones undergoing changes were said to be not at equilibrium.

During the last few minutes of class, several of the pupils took turns disturbing the systems away from equilibrium. They wound up the toys, turned on the flashlight, stretched the spring and then released it, picked the rock out of the water and dropped it back, and agitated the water in the glass containing the sugar crystals. Their actions suggested that they thought of equilibrium mainly in terms of mechanical motion and rest.

The fact that agitating the sugar water hastens the solution process while it disturbs mechanical equilibrium was not clear to them. The equilibrium concept has to be extended in the future.

Reversibility and Irreversibility: One of the rules that has no exception in our experience is that undisturbed systems tend to come to an equilibrium with their environment. The ice cube in the warm room melts, the drop of water in the refrigerator freezes; the pendulum oscillates with smaller and smaller amplitude until it comes to rest. Because the rule has no exceptions, no one is conscious of the fact that all natural processes are irreversible: the puddle of water in the glass in the room does not freeze into an ice cube, the rusty water does not separate into a nail and clean water, the pendulum does not start swinging with larger and larger amplitude in the absence of external intervention.

Even though the second grader will not be ready for some time to analyze why this rule holds and in what unusual circumstances it has exceptions, the second grader is ready to become aware of the rule. He can learn to observe phenomena with sufficient care so as to distinguish irreversible ones from reversible ones.

The teaching procedure was based on the use of a motion picture projector that could be operated forward or backward. The question of reversibility was then rephrased as follows: Could the audience tell whether the projector was being run forward or backward? If the audience could tell, then the scene showed an irreversible process; if the audience could not tell, then the scene showed a process that was reversible as far as the available information revealed. Actually, there are no truly reversible macroscopic processes; nevertheless short excerpts of film that do not show the beginning and end of an experiment often appear reversible. A film of an egg falling could have been taken of an egg falling (film run normally) or of an egg that was thrown up into the air (film run in reverse). That is a reversible part of the experiment. The impact of the egg, however, is clearly irreversible.

The idea of the distinction between reversible and irreversible processes was introduced by showing the pupils a film composed of reversible and irreversible scenes. The film was run in both directions. When it was run backwards, many of the scenes looked "funny" and aroused great merriment among the children. In the second lesson, the sense of operation of the projector was switched frequently and the children were asked to state whether the film was running normally or reversed. As expected, the answers were unanimous on the irreversible scenes and divided on the reversible ones. In the third lesson, the film and also real processes in the classroom and at home were analyzed for reversibility. For instance, the children considered faking the movie of a person jumping into a swimming pool. They suggested that one make a movie of a person walking in a pool that had thumbtacks on the floor. That person would jump out! Then one could run the movie backwards. In the fourth lesson of the series, each child was invited to act out a scene in front of a movie camera. He had to plan the scene to be reversible or very irreversible, as he wished. The children's performance indicated that they could make the distinction quite well, even though subtleties in the motion of their clothes escaped them. In the last lesson the class reviewed the movies they had made to approve of or to criticize the scenes thought up by the children.

Relativity of Position and Motion: The basis of this series of lessons has been described near the end of the section on major science concepts. A description of the classroom procedures that were used in teaching is contained in the separate article entitled "Meet Mr. O" (26).

Conclusion

In this article I have outlined a science teaching program which has as its objective the advancement of scientific literacy. The program is based on certain ideas as to the nature of science and the nature of the learning process, ideas that have been taken from the work of others. It appears that the expectations and interpretations of scientists play a decisive role in the discovery of new knowledge; the raw observations are as important, but are not usable in the absence of a conceptual framework with which their significance can be evaluated. It appears also that verbal labels play an extremely important role in enabling children to discriminate between concepts. In the science program, these two findings are combined systematically in an attempt to teach the pupils to look at natural phenomena from a scientific point of view.

Once the beginnings have been made with the fundamental concepts of material objects, systems, interactions and relativity, the pupils should be able to assimilate their experiences in later science classes and outside school into this conceptual framework. They will then be able to benefit from individual experiments they carry out with less and less guidance as they become older. In high school, finally, the students will be able to take advantage of opportunities for designing and carrying out independent investigations. The students will also be able to understand the development of science, in which more primitive concepts based on a narrow range of experience were gradually replaced by more modern concepts that deal with a broader range of experience. In this way the high school graduate will have assimilated the conceptual structure of science, will have had some firsthand research experience, and will have some historical perspective; I think he then can be called scientifically literate.

References

1. C. P. Snow. *The Two Cultures and the Scientific Revolution.* New York: Cambridge University Press, 1959.
2. Morris H. Shamos. "Science and Common Sense." *The Science Teacher* 29: 7-11; September 1962.
3. Robert Karplus. "Beginning a Study in Elementary School Science." *American Journal of Physics* 30; 1962.
4. Robert Karplus. "The Science Curriculum—One Approach." *Elementary School Journal* 62: 243-52; 1962.
5. Lloyd F. Scott. "An Experiment in Teaching Basic Science in the Elementary School." *Science Education* 46: 105-108; 1962.
6. Lloyd F. Scott. "The University of California Elementary School Science Project: A Two-Year Report." *Science Education* 46: 109-13; 1962.
7. Robert Karplus. *Coordinates.* Elementary School Science Project. Berkeley: University of California, 1959.
8. Robert Karplus. *Force.* Elementary School Science Project. Berkeley: University of California, 1959.
9. Jean Piaget. *The Child's Conception of Physical Reality.* New York: Humanities Press, 1951.
10. Bärbel Inhelder and Jean Piaget. *The Growth of Logical Thinking from Childhood to Adolescence.* New York: Basic Books, 1958.
11. Louise Boehm. "Exploring Children's Thinking." *Elementary School Journal* 61: 363-73; 1961.
12. Celia B. Stendler. "Elementary Teaching and the Piagetian Theory." *The Science Teacher* 29: 34-39; September 1962.
13. *A Program for Teaching Science.* Thirty-first Yearbook of the National Society for the Study of Education, Part 1. Chicago: Distributed by the University of Chicago Press, 1932.
14. *Science Education in American Schools.* Forty-sixth Yearbook of the National Society for the Study of Education, Part 1. Chicago: Distributed by the University of Chicago Press, 1947.
15. *Rethinking Science Education.* Fifty-ninth Yearbook of the National Society for the Study of Education, Part 1. Chicago: Distributed by the University of Chicago Press, 1960.
16. Jerome S. Bruner. *The Process of Education.* Cambridge, Massachusetts: Harvard University Press, 1960.
17. Thomas Kuhn. *The Nature of Scientific Revolutions.* Chicago: University of Chicago Press, 1962.
18. Karl Popper. *The Logic of Scientific Discovery.* New York: Basic Books, 1959.
19. Information about innovations in high school science teaching can be obtained from:
   Educational Services Incorporated, 108 Water Street, Watertown, Massachusetts.
   Biological Sciences Curriculum Study, University of Colorado, Boulder, Colorado.
   CBA Chemistry, Earlham College, Richmond, Indiana.

CHEM Study, University of California, Berkeley 4, California.

20. David P. Ausubel. "Implications of Preadolescent and Early Adolescent Cognitive Development for Secondary School Teaching." Urbana, Illinois: Bureau of Educational Research, University of Illinois, 1961.

21. Celia B. Stendler. "Cognitive Development in Children and Readiness for High School Physics." *American Journal of Physics* 12: 832-35; 1961.

22. From *Language, Thought and Reality, Selected Writings of Benjamin Lee Whorf.* Cambridge, Massachusetts: The M.I.T. Press, Massachusetts Institute of Technology, 1956. p. 209.

23. L. S. Vygotsky. *Thought and Language.* Cambridge, Massachusetts: The Technology Press, Massachusetts Institute of Technology, 1962.

24. Millie Almy. "What Can Children Learn in Nursery School?" *Journal of Nursery Education* 17: 137-40; May 1962.

25. A further refinement is described by J. M. Atkin and R. Karplus in "Discovery or Invention?" *The Science Teacher* 29: 45-51; September 1962.

26. Robert Karplus. "Meet Mr. O." *Science and Children* 1: 19-24; November 1963.

The Formation of Mathematical Concepts in Primary-Grade Children

THE aims of this paper are primarily constructive, that is, to contribute to the development of a scientific theory of concept formation. However, before turning to this subject, there are two general aspects of the teaching of mathematical concepts upon which I want to comment.[1]

Teaching of Mathematical Concepts

The first concerns the much heard remark that the newer revisions of the mathematics curriculum are particularly significant because of the emphasis they are placing on *understanding* concepts as opposed to the perfection of *rote* skills. My point is not to disagree with this remark, but to urge that it is essentially banal. It is a good thing to understand; it is a bad thing to possess mere rote skill. The banality arises from not knowing what we mean by *understanding*. This failure is not due to disagreement over whether the test of understanding should be a behavioral one. I am inclined to think that most people concerned with this matter would admit the central relevance of overt behavior as a measure of understanding. The difficulty is rather that no one seems to be very clear about the exact specification of the behavior required to exhibit understanding. Moreover, apart even from any behavioral questions the very notion of understanding seems fundamentally vague and ill-defined.

[1] This research has been supported by the United States Office of Education, Department of Health, Education and Welfare, the National Science Foundation and the Carnegie Corporation of New York.

To illustrate what I mean, let us suppose that we can talk about understanding in some general way. Consider now the concept of triangularity. Does understanding this concept entail understanding that the sum of the interior angles is 180°, or that triangles are rigid whereas quadrilaterals are not, or being able to prove that if the bisectors of two angles of a triangle are equal then the triangle is isosceles? This example suggests one classical philosophical response to our query, namely, to understand a concept means, it is said, to know or to believe as true a certain set of propositions that use the concept.

Unfortunately, this set is badly defined. It is trivial to remark that along these lines we might work out a comparative notion of understanding that is a partial ordering defined in terms of the inclusion relation among sets of propositions that use the concept. Thus one person understands the concept of triangularity better than a second if the set of propositions that use the concept and that are known to the first person includes the corresponding set for the second person. (Notice that it will not do to say simply that the first person knows more propositions using the concept, for the second person might know fewer propositions but among these would be some of the more profound propositions not known by the first person; this situation corresponds to the widely held and probably correct belief that the deepest mathematicians are not necessarily the best mathematical scholars.)

Yet this partial ordering does not take us very far. A more behavioral line of thought that at first glance may seem more promising is the response of the advocates of programed learning to the charge that the learning of programed material facilitates rote skills but not genuine understanding of concepts. The response is to assert that if the critics will simply specify the behavior they regard as providing evidence of understanding, they, the programers, will guarantee to develop and perfect the appropriate repertoire of responses. This approach has the practical virtue of sidestepping any complex discussion of understanding, and supposes, with considerable correctness, no doubt, that without giving an intellectually exact analysis of what it means to understand a concept, we still can obtain a rough consensus at any given time as to what body of propositions we expect students to master about a given concept. This is the appropriate practical engineering approach, but it scarcely touches the scientific problem.

In this paper I do not pretend to offer any serious characterization of what it means to understand a concept. I do think that the most promising direction is to develop a psychological theory of concept transfer and generalization. The still relatively primitive state of the theory of the much simpler phenomena of stimulus transfer and generalization does not make me optimistic about the immediate future. For immediate purposes, however, let me sketch in a very rough way how the application of ideas of transfer and generalization can be used to attack the banality mentioned earlier in the standard dichotomy of understanding versus rote skill. We would all agree, I think, that such matters as learning to give the multiplication tables quickly and with accuracy are indeed rote skills. Yet there is also what I consider to be a mistaken tendency to extend the label "rote skill" to many parts of the traditional mathematics curriculum at all levels. The body of mathematical material tested, for example, by the British Sixth Form examinations is sometimes so labeled by advocates of the newer mathematics curriculum. In terms of the accepted notion of rote skill developed and studied by psychologists, this is a mistake, for the production of a correct response on these examinations cannot be explained by any simple principles of stimulus-response association. Moreover, the problems of transfer involved in solving typical British Sixth Form examination problems in comparison with the kind of examination set by advocates of the newer mathematics curriculum may in fact require more transfer of concepts—at least more transfer in one obvious way of measuring transfer, that is, in terms of the number of hours of training spent in relation to the ability to solve the problems on the part of students matched as to general background and ability. I recognize that these are complicated matters and I do not want to pursue them here. Also I am fully in sympathy with the general objectives of the newer mathematics curriculum. I am simply protesting here against some of the remarks about understanding and rote skills that occur in the pedagogical conversations and writing of mathematicians.

A second general point relates to the many current discussions of the efficacy of the discovery method of teaching. The discussions of this method seem to provide yet one more remarkable example in the history of education of a viewpoint coming to prominence without any serious body of empirical evidence to support or refute its advocates. From the standpoint of learning theory I do not even know of a relatively systematic definition of the discovery method. I do not doubt that some of the advocates of this method are themselves remarkably capable teachers and are able to do unusual and startling things with classes of elementary school children.

The intellectual problem, however, is to separate the pedagogical virtuosities of personality of these advocates from the systematic problem of analyzing the method itself. Workable hypotheses need to be formulated and tested. I know that it is a standard objection of some advocates of the discovery method that any quick laboratory examination of this teaching method versus a more standard immediate reinforcement method, particularly as applied to young children, is bound not to yield an unbiased test. The results and the implications of the method, it is said, can only be properly evaluated after a long period. I personally rather doubt that this is the case but, if it is so, or if it is propounded as a working hypothesis by advocates of the method, then it seems to me that it is their intellectual responsibility to formulate proper tests of a sufficiently sustained sort. I realize that my remarks on this subject in this paper have the character of *obiter dicta*. On the other hand, in a more complete treatment of mathematical concept formation in young children, I would consider it necessary to probe more deeply into the issues of motivation, reinforcement and concept formation surrounding the controversy between the discovery method and other more classical methods of reinforcement.

I turn now to specific topics I would like to develop more systematically. In the next section an intuitive version of stimulus-sampling learning theory is sketched; it is this theory we have attempted to apply to the experiments dealing with mathematical concept formation in young children described in the following section. A description of these experiments is concluded by attempting to summarize some of the more important findings from the standpoint of pedagogical practice.

In the final section I give a brief description of the related pedagogical program in elementary-school mathematics. It should be emphasized that the empirical variables considered in the experiments have not been arbitrarily selected. The experimental program has been carried out concurrently with the development of a program of primary-grade mathematics, "Sets and Numbers," which makes use of simple set-theoretical notions to introduce the child at the outset to concepts and operations of arithmetic. A concept to be learned in each experiment and the experimental variables introduced have some bearing on problems which have arisen in the development of the Sets and Numbers program.

Sketch of Stimulus-Sampling Learning Theory

In paradigmatic form the theory was developed for an experimental situation in which a subject is presented on each trial with some stimulus display to which he is required to make a specific response. The subject is always told whether he is correct or incorrect on that trial.

The basic assumption of the theory is that in such a situation the correct response will become associated with, or conditioned to, the stimulus display. If it is conditioned, the subject will continue to respond correctly whenever the same stimulus is presented. On the other hand, when the correct response is not conditioned to a stimulus display, the probability of a correct response is at some chance level which remains constant until the association between the stimulus and appropriate response has been established.

More generally, the postulated sequence of events occurring on a given trial in an experiment may be described as follows: The organism begins the trial in a certain state of conditioning. Among the stimuli available a certain set is sampled. On the basis of this sampled stimuli and their conditioning connections to the possible responses, the response is made. After the response is made, a reinforcement occurs which may change the conditioning of the sampled stimuli. The organism then enters a new state of conditioning ready for the next trial.

In the experiments to be described here we shall apply the theory in a simple fashion by postulating that there is exactly one stimulus element available for sampling on each trial and that at the beginning of the experiment this single element is unconditioned. This special one-element model has been applied with considerable success to paired-associate experiments, that is, to experiments in which the subject must learn an arbitrary association established by the experimenter between, say, a nonsense-syllable of a single stimulus and the response such as one of the numerals, 1 to 8, or by the pressing of one of three keys. The most important psychological implication of this one-element model of the theory is that in the paired-associate situation the conditioning takes place on an all-or-none basis. This means that prior to conditioning the organism is simply guessing the correct response with a fixed probability. Once the stimulus is conditioned the correct response is made with probability one. The kind of learning described with this model is often referred to as insightful learning or the "ah ha" experience. I believe it is important to emphasize that learning of this qualitative character can be given an exact quantitative formulation within stimulus-response theory.

In an earlier paper Rose Ginsberg and I (1963) analyzed a number of experiments, including some of those reported here, to exhibit a simple but fundamentally important fact about this all-or-none conditioning model. The assumptions of the model imply that the sequence of correct and incorrect responses prior to the last error form a binomial distribution of Bernoulli trials with parameter p. This null hypothesis of a fixed binomial distribution of responses prior to the last error admits at once the possibility of applying many powerful classical statistics that are not usually applicable to learning data. What is particularly important from a psychological standpoint is the implication of this hypothesis that the mean learning curve, when estimated over responses prior to the last error, will be a horizontal line. In other words, no effects of learning should be shown prior to conditioning. Ginsberg and I analyzed experiments concerned with children's concept formation, animal learning, probability learning and paired-associate learning in adults from this standpoint. I shall not propose to give as extensive analysis of data in the present paper as we attempted there. I will, however, attempt to cite some of the results on the question of stationarity because of its fundamental importance for any psychological evaluation of the kind of processes by which young children acquire concepts.

Other features of the experiments summarized in the following pages will be mentioned seriatim, particularly if they have some bearing on pedagogical questions. There is, however, one general methodological point that should be mentioned before individual experiments are described. In many of the experiments described the stimulus displays were different on every trial, so that there was no possibility of establishing a simple stimulus-response association. How is the one-element model to be applied to such data? The answer represents, I think, one of our more important general findings. It is that a very good account of much of the data may be obtained by treating the concept itself as the single element. The schema is then that a simple concept-response association is established. Except for Experiment I, it is with this interpretation that we have applied the one-element model to our experiments.

Experiment I. Binary Numbers

This experiment is reported in detail in Suppes and Ginsberg (1962b). Five- and six-year-old subjects were required to learn the concepts of the numbers 4 and 5 in the binary number system, each concept being represented by three different stimuli; for example, if the stimuli had been chosen from the Roman alphabet, as in fact they were not, 4 could have been represented by abb, cdd and eff, and 5 by aba, cdc and efe. The child was required to respond by placing directly upon the stimulus one of two cards. On one card was inscribed a large Arabic numeral 4 and on the other a large Arabic numeral 5. All the children were told on each trial whether they made the correct or incorrect response, but half of them were also required to *correct* their responses following an error.

Thus in this experiment in addition to testing the one-element model, we were concerned to examine the effect upon learning of requiring the subject to correct overtly a wrong response. There were 24 subjects in each of the two experimental groups. From test responses, after each experimental session, it seemed evident that whereas some subjects in both groups learned the concept as such, others learned only some of the specific stimuli representing the concepts, so that in effect within each group there were two subgroups of subjects. It is interesting to note that this finding is in agreement with some similar results in lower organisms (Hull and Spence, 1938), but contrary to results obtained with adult subjects, for whom an overt correction response seems to have negligible behavioral effects (Burke, Estes and Hellyer, 1954).

The data for both correction and noncorrection groups show that there was a significant difference between the two groups in the rate of learning. The t of 4.00 computed between overall responses of the two groups is significant at the .001 level.

For the analysis of paired-associates and concept formation we restricted ourselves to the 24 subjects of the correction group. To begin with, we analyzed the data as if each of the six stimuli, three for each number, represented an independent paired-associate item. Because a total of only 16 trials were run on each stimulus we adopted a criterion of six successive correct responses and thus the proportion of correct responses prior to the last error was examined only for the first ten trials. An X^2 test of stationarity over blocks of single trials supports the null hypothesis ($X^2 = 8.00$, df $=9$, P$> .50$, N$=844$).

Let us now turn to the question of concept formation. The identification we make has already been indicated. We treat the concept as itself the single stimulus, and in this case we regard the experiment as consisting of two concepts, one for the number 4 and one for the number 5. (It should be apparent that the identification in terms of the numbers 4 and 5 is not necessary; each concept can be viewed simply as an abstract pattern.)

Using as the criterion that the concept had been learned if the responses to the last three presentations of each stimuli represented were correct, we divided the data into two parts. The data from the group meeting the criterion were arranged for concept learning analysis, in this case a two-item learning situation. The remaining data were assumed to represent paired-associate learning involving six independent stimulus items. For the paired-associate group over the first 10 trials we had 81 cases. For the concept-formation group we had 21 cases with 48 trials in each. The X^2 test of stationarity was not significant for either group (for the concept subgroup $X^2 = 8.36$, df $= 9$, P $> .30$, N $= 357$; for the paired-associate subgroup $X^2 = 11.26$, df $= 8$, P $> .10$, N $= 570$).

To provide a more delicate analysis of this important question of stationarity we can construct Vincent curves (cf. Suppes and Ginsberg, 1963). The proportion of correct responses prior to the last error may be tabulated for percentiles of trials instead of in terms of the usual blocks of trials. There was some evidence of non-stationarity in the final quartile.

It should be noted, of course, that the subjects who take longer to reach criterion are weighted more heavily in the Vincent curves. For example, suppose one subject has sixteen responses prior to his last error whereas another subject has four responses prior to his last error. The first subject contributes four responses to each quartile whereas the second subject contributes only one. Let us turn now to the second experiment.

This experiment was performed with Rose Ginsberg, and we have published some of the results in Suppes and Ginsberg (1963) but the detailed report of the experiment has not yet appeared. The learning tasks involved in this experiment were equivalence of sets and the two related concepts of identity of sets and identity of ordered sets.

Ninety-six first grade subjects were run, in four groups of twenty-four each. In Group 1 the subjects were required to learn identity of sets for 56 trials and then equivalence for a further 56 trials. In Group 1 this order of presentation was reversed. In Group 3 the subjects learned first identity of ordered sets and then identity of sets. In Group 4 identity of sets preceded identity of ordered sets. Following our findings in Experiment I, that is, that learning was more rapid when the child was required to make an overt correction response after an error, we included this requirement in Experiment II and most of the subsequent experiments reported here. Also in this experiment and those reported later in this paper as well, no stimulus display on any trial was repeated for an individual subject. This was done in order to guarantee that the learning of the concept could not be explained by any simple principles of stimulus-response association, as was the case for Experiment I. For convenience of reference we have termed concept experiments in which no stimulus display is repeated *pure* property or *pure* concept experiments.

The sets depicted by the stimulus displays consisted of one, two or three elements. On each trial two of these sets were displayed. Minimal instructions were given the subjects to press one of two buttons when the stimulus pairs presented were "the same" and the alternative button when they were "not the same."

Our empirical aims in this experiment were several. First, we wanted to examine in detail whether the learning of simple set concepts by children of this age took place on an all-or-none conditioning basis. Secondly, as the two sequences of learning trials on two different concepts for each group would indicate, we were interested in questions of transfer. Would the learning of one kind of concept facilitate the learning of another, and were there significant differences in the degree of this facilitation? Thirdly, we were concerned to consider the question of finding the behavioral level at which the concepts could be most adequately defined. For example, in learning the identity of sets could the learning trials be satisfactorily analyzed from the standpoint of all trials falling under a single concept? Would it be better to separate the trials on which identical sets were presented from those on which nonidentical sets were presented in order to analyze the data in terms of two concepts? Or would a still finer division of concepts be called for in terms of sets identical in terms of order (O), sets identical as non-ordered sets ($I\overline{O}$), equivalent sets ($E\overline{I}$) and non-equivalent sets?

In somewhat summary fashion the experimental results were as follows: First, the relevant mean learning curves showed that the number of errors on the concept of identity of ordered sets was extremely small. From the high proportion of correct responses even in the first block of trials of this concept it was evident that this is a very natural and simple concept for children.

Learning curves for trials before the last error were also constructed for all groups. To identify the last error prior to conditioning, we adopted a criterion of 16 successive correct responses. The combined curve for Groups 1a and 4a was clearly stationary. This was also the case for 3a, 4b, 2b and 3b. The results of the X^2 test of stationarity for blocks of 4 trials are shown in Table 1 and confirm these graphic observations. Only the curve for 1b approached significance. (No computation was made for 3a because of the small number of errors; the number of subjects in the final block of 4 trials is shown in the right-hand column of the table.)

Table 1. Stationarity Results for Equivalence and Identity of Sets Experiment (Experiment II)

Group	X^2	df	P >	Ss in last block
1a & 4a	4.95	9	.80	9
1b	16.69	9	.05	12
2a	4.79	9	.80	11
3a	—— Too few errors ——			1
4b	4.89	9	.80	5
2b	5.96	9	.70	5
3b	3.49	9	.90	10

I shall restrict myself to one Vincent curve for this experiment. The 48 subjects of Groups 1 and 4 began with the concept of identity of sets. Of the 48 subjects, 38 met the criterion of 16 successive correct responses mentioned above. The Vincent curve for the criterion subjects showed evidence of non-stationarity in the fourth quartile, as in the case of Experiment I.

From examination of the mean learning curves over all trials, there seemed to be little evidence of transfer. And somewhat surprisingly, the only definite evidence confirmed the existence of negative transfer. The effects of transfer are actually more evident when we examine the data from the standpoint of 2 or 4 concepts. Here I shall try to summarize only what appear to be the most important points. For learning of identity of sets, prior training on equivalence has positive transfer for class $I\overline{O}$ (pairs of sets identical only in the sense of unordered sets) and negative transfer for $\overline{EI}$ (pairs of sets that are equivalent but not identical). The qualitative explanation seems obvious. The initial natural dichotomy seems to be O, $\overline{O}$, and for this dichotomy $I\overline{O}$ is a class of "different" pairs, but the task of equivalence reinforces the treatment of $I\overline{O}$ pairs as the "same." The situation is reversed for the class $\overline{EI}$, and thus the negative transfer for under equivalence $\overline{EI}$ pairs are the "same," but under identity of sets they are "different."

When (3b) the task is again identity of sets but the prior training is on identity of ordered sets rather than equivalence, there is, as would be expected by the kind of argument just given, negative transfer for the class $I\overline{O}$. There is also some slight evidence of positive transfer for $\overline{EI}$.

From the data of Groups 2a and 1b, we inferred positive transfer for the class $I\overline{O}$ when the task is equivalence and the prior training is on identity of sets. What is surprising is the relatively slight amount of negative transfer for the class $\overline{EI}$.

Finally comparing Groups 3a and 4b, we observed negative transfer for the class $I\overline{O}$, as would be expected. The response curves for the other three classes are too close to probability one to make additional inferences, although there is a slight negative transfer for $\overline{EI}$ which cannot be explained on the principles stated above.

It seems apparent from these results that the analysis of transfer in the learning of mathematical concepts may often be facilitated if a fine-scale breakdown of the concepts in question into a number of subconcepts is possible. What is most needed is a quantitative theory to guide a more detailed analysis of the transfer phenomena.

Experiment III. Polygons and Angles

This experiment is reported in detail in Stoll (1962), and I present some of the data here with her permission. The subjects were 32 kindergarten children who were divided into two equal groups. For both groups the experiment was a successive discrimination, three-response situation, with one group discriminating between triangles, quadrilaterals and pentagons, and the other group discriminating between acute, right and obtuse angles. For all subjects a typical case of each form (*i.e.*, one of the three types of polygons or three types of angles) was shown immediately above the appropriate response key. As in the case of Experiment II, no single stimulus display was repeated for any one subject. Stimulus displays representing each form were randomized over experimental trials in blocks of nine, with three of each type appearing in each block of nine. The subjects were run to a criterion of nine successively correct responses, but with not more than 54 trials in any one session.

Table 2. Stationarity Order and Binomial Distribution Results (Stoll Experiment on Geometric Forms)

	X^2	df	P >
Quadrilateral, p = .609			
Stationarity (N = 273)	1.68	4	.70
Order (N = 262)	0.65	1	.40
Binomial distribution (N = 65)	1.77	2	.40
Pentagon, p = .600			
Stationarity (N = 275)	2.40	4	.60
Order (N = 269)	1.76	1	.15
Binomial distribution (N = 65)	2.07	2	.35
Acute angle, p = .674			
Stationarity (N = 338)	7.96	4	.05
Order (N = 348)	3.17	1	.05
Binomial distribution (N = 85)	2.66	2	.25
Right angle, p. = .506			
Stationarity (N = 313)	6.34	4	.10
Order (N = 326)	2.41	1	.10
Binomial distribution (N = 80)	10.52	2	.001
Obtuse angle, p = .721			
Stationarity (N = 268)	1.10	4	.85
Order (N = 256)	7.32	1	.001
Binomial distribution (N = 63)	2.90	2	.20
Quadrilateral and pentagon, p = .604			
Stationarity (N = 548)	0.71	4	.90
Binomial distribution (N = 130)	1.77	2	.40
All angles, p = .624			
Stationarity (N = 919)	0.97	4	.90

I omit data for the triangles because only a small number of errors were made.

The pentagons, quadrilaterals and right angles had quite stationary Vincent curves, whereas there was a definite increase in the fourth quartile of the Vincent curves for the acute and obtuse angles, and in fact in the case of the obtuse angles a significant increase in the third quartile. Statistical tests of stationarity of these Vincent curves support these results of visual inspection. Each test has three degrees of freedom because the analysis is based on the data for the four quartiles. In the case of the quadrilaterals $X^2 = 1.75$, for the pentagons $X^2 = 1.33$, for the right angles $X^2 = .95$, for the obtuse angles $X^2 = 12.63$, and for the acute angles $X^2 = 16.43$. Only the last two values are significant.

Using responses before the last error, for all concepts except that of a triangle, goodness-of-fit tests were performed for (a) stationarity in blocks of 6 trials, (b) binomial distribution of responses as correct or incorrect in blocks of 4 trials, and (c) independence of responses — with the test being for zero-order vs. first-order dependence. The results of these facts are presented in Table 2 (page 109). The results shown strongly support the adequacy of the one-element model for this experiment.

Experiment IV. Variation in Method of Stimulus Display

In this study conducted with Rose Ginsberg we compared the rate of learning in two experimental situations, one in which stimulus displays were presented individually in the usual way and the other in which the same stimulus displays were presented by means of colored slides to groups of four children. The concept to be learned was identity of sets, and in both situations the children were required to respond by pressing one of two buttons, depending upon whether the stimulus display on that trial was identical or nonidentical. Of the 64 subjects 32 were from first grade and 32 from kindergarten classes. For the children receiving individual displays the experimental situation was essentially identical with that of Experiment II.

However, each group was divided into two subgroups. One subgroup received the stimulus material in random order, and the other in an order based on anticipated difficulty, in particular, with presentations of one-element sets coming first, then two-element sets and finally three-element sets.

Analysis of the mean learning curves for the two subgroups with random presentation indicated that presentations by slides are a less effective learning device for younger children, and the younger the child the more this finding seems to apply. At all levels of difficulty the kindergarten children learned more efficiently when the stimuli were presented to them in individual sessions. With one- or two-element sets displayed, Grade 1 subjects learned only slightly better in the individual session situation than in the slide situation, but when the task was more difficult (stimulus displays of three-element sets) the individual learning situation was clearly the most adequate. In interpreting these results it should be emphasized that the individual session was strictly experimental so that the amount of interaction between subject and experimenter was paralleled in both individual and slide situations.

Why these two experimental situations should produce different results in terms of efficiency of learning is not yet clear to us. One possibility is the following. It has been shown both with lower organisms (Murphy and Miller, 1955) and with young children (Murphy and Miller, 1959) that the ideal situation for learning is when the stimulus, response and reinforcement are contiguous. In the individual sessions these requirements were met, for the response buttons were 1.5 inches below the stimulus displays and the reinforcement lights were 1.0 inch from the stimuli. On the other hand, in the slide presentations, although the stimulus displays and reinforcements were immediately adjacent to each other, the response buttons were about 3 ft. from the screen on which the stimulus display was projected. Experimentally it has been shown (Murphy and Miller, 1959) that with children of this age group a separation of 6.0 inches is sufficient to interfere with efficient learning.

Experiment V. Incidental Learning

This experiment represents a joint study with Rose Ginsberg. Thirty-six kindergarten children in three groups of 12 each were run for 60 trials a day on two successive days of individual experimental sessions during which they were required to learn equivalence of sets. On the first day the stimulus displays presented to the subjects on each trial differed in color between the three groups but were otherwise the same. In Group 1 all displays were in one color, black. In Group 2 equivalence sets were presented in red and nonequivalence sets in yellow. For the first 12 trials in Group 3, equivalent sets were in red and nonequivalent sets in yellow; for the remaining 48 trials on that day the two colors were gradually fused until discrimination between them was not possible. On the second day all sets were presented to all three groups in one color, black.

As is apparent from the brief description of the experimental design, Group 1 simply had two days' practice under the same conditions with the concept of equivalence. In Group 2 the child did not actually need to learn the concept of equivalence but he could simply respond to the color difference on the first day, and it is well known that such a color discrimination for young children is a simple task. If the child in this group learned anything about equivalence of sets the first day, therefore, we may assume this to be a function of incidental learning. If incidental learning is effective, his performance on the second day when the color cue is dropped should at least be better than the performance of children in Group 1 on the first day. In Group 3 where we give the child the discriminative cue of color difference in the first trial and then very slowly withdraw that cue, the child should continue to search the stimulus displays very closely for a color stimulus, and is thus obliged to pay very close attention to the stimuli.

Analysis of the mean learning curves for the three groups indicated that of the three groups, only Group 2 approached perfect learning on the first day. In this group, of course, only color discrimination was necessary. Both the other groups did not improve over the first 60 trials, although

Group 3 showed some initial improvement over those trials when the color cues remained discriminable. On the second day Group 1 showed no improvement, and the learning curves for this group and for Group 2 are practically identical. For Group 3 on the other hand, the results were conspicuously better on the second day than for those of any other group. It was apparent from the learning curves that the task chosen was relatively difficult for the age of the children, because essentially no improvement was shown by Group 1 over the entire 120 trials. The conditions in Group 3 in which the children were forced to pay very close attention to the stimuli, do seem to have significantly enhanced the learning.

Experiment VI. Variation of Response Methods

This study was made jointly with Rose Ginsberg, and its object was to study the behavioral effects of different methods of response. Specifically, three groups, each composed of 20 kindergarten children, were taken individually through a sequence of 60 trials on each of two successive days for a total of 120 trials. The task for all three groups was equivalence of sets.

In Group 1 the child was presented with pictures of two sets of objects and indicated by pressing one of two buttons whether the sets "went together" or did not "go together" (were equivalent or nonequivalent).

In Group 2 the child was presented with one display set and two "answer" sets and was required to choose the answer which "went together" with the display set.

In Group 3 the child was presented with one display set and three "answer" sets and made his choice from the three possible answers.

This situation has fairly direct reference to teaching methodology in the sense that Group 2 and Group 3 represent multiple-choice possibilities. In Group 1, in which the child is required to identify either the presence of the concept or its absence on each trial, the situation is comparable to one in which the child is to indicate whether an equation or statement is correct or incorrect.

On the first day each group of children learned the task described above. On the second day they were run on an alternative method. Specifically, Group 1 was run under Group 3 conditions and Groups 2 and 3 were run under Group 1 conditions.

Analysis of the mean learning curves for all groups on both days indicated that in Group 2, where the subjects were required to choose from one or two available responses, the subjects learned slightly more quickly and to a slightly better level of achievement on Day 1 than the other groups, but, on the second day, when the experimental conditions were shifted, Group 2 subjects did less well than the subjects in the other two groups. The clear superiority of Group 1 on the second day, when they were transferred to Group 3 conditions, indicated some positive transfer from learning to judge whether or not a concept is present to the multiple-choice situation, whereas the results for Groups 2 and 3 on the second day indicated some negative transfer from the multiple-response methods to the presence-or-absence method.

These results are further supported when we examine separately the data from subjects achieving a criterion of 12 successive correct responses on the first day. The more successful method was clearly that used in Group 1. The subjects in this group were conspicuously more successful than the other groups on the second day, making, in fact, no errors on that day from Trial 30 to Trial 60. Group 3 achieved perfect scores on the second day only on the last six trials, and Group 2 never reached that level on the second day, although they, like the other criterion subjects, had achieved perfect learning on the first day.

It seems reasonable tentatively to conclude that the method used with Group 1, in which subjects were required to recognize the presence or absence of some property on each trial, is the more successful method in establishing understanding of a concept well enough to permit transfer to a different response method.

Support for the all-or-none model of conditioning is also to be found in this experiment. In Table 3, X^2 goodness-of-fit tests of stationarity over trials before the final error for each group on each day are shown. The six values are all non-significant and thus support the basic assumption of the all-or-none models.

Table 3. Test for Stationarity over Trials before the Final Error (Experiment VI)

	Group 1		Group 2		Group 3	
	Day 1	Day 2	Day 1	Day 2	Day 1	Day 2
X^2	4.97	2.41	10.76	4.255	16.07	2.87
df	8	1	9	8	9	7
P >	.70	.10	.20	.80	.05	.80

On the basis of the six experiments just discussed I would like to draw some tentative conclusions, some of which are important for pedagogical procedures (cf. Suppes and Ginsberg, 1962a). I want to emphasize, however, that I would not wish to claim that the evidence from these experiments is conclusive enough to establish any one of the six conclusions in any final way, but what I do hope is that the attempt to summarize some of the implications of these experiments will stimulate other research workers to investigate these and related propositions in more adequate detail.

1. Formation of simple mathematical concepts in young children is approximately an all-or-none process. Evidence indicates, however, that significant deviations from the all-or-none model are present.

2. Learning is more efficient if the child who makes an error is required to make an overt correction response in the presence of the stimulus to be learned (Experiment I).

3. Incidental learning does not appear to be an effective method of acquisition for young children and in Experiment IV the group of children who responded to a color discrimination did not subsequently give any indication of having learned the underlying concepts.

4. Contiguity of response, stimulus and reinforcement enhances learning (Experiment V).

5. In the learning of related mathematical concepts, the amount of overall transfer from the learning of one concept to another is surprisingly small. However, considerable positive or negative transfer between specific sub-concepts is often present (Experiment II).

6. Transfer of a concept is more effective if the learning situation has required the subject to recognize the presence or absence of a concept in a number of stimulus displays than if learning has involved matching from a number of possible responses (Experiment VI).

Several of these conclusions are at variance with generally accepted results for adult learning behavior, for example, the efficacy of an immediate overt correction response (see Burke, Estes and Hellyer, 1954, for negative results on this method in adults), the variation of response method, or the relative specificity of learning of concepts with relatively little transfer. What is much needed is a wider range of systematic studies to isolate the factors of learning in young children that are particularly distinct from common features of adult learning behavior.

Sets and Numbers Pedagogical Program

All mathematics can be developed from the notions of sets and operations upon sets. The study of sets would therefore seem to provide the ideal initial introduction to mathematics but is ordinarily considered too "abstract" to introduce early in the student's development. The term "set" is in fact a simple concrete term—easy both to explain and understand. A set is simply any collection or family of objects. Thus, we may speak of the set or collection of all students now in the first grade, the set or collection of dolls now owned by Mary Jones, the set or collection of all Irishmen, the set or collection of all cowboys. The method of displaying problems by grouping objects as used in the standard workbooks approaches the set notion, but the lack of an explicit notation makes precise definitions difficult, if not impossible. Our empirical findings indicate that simple mathematical concepts can be understood by the beginner provided that these are presented precisely with the help of a consistent notation.

There are at least two major reasons to begin first grade arithmetic with the explicit introduction of the notion of set and appropriate notation for sets and operations upon them. In the first place, sets are more concrete objects than numbers. At the same time operations upon sets are more meaningful to the student than manipulation of numbers. The putting together of sets of physical objects, for example, is a more concrete operation than the addition of numbers. The many exercises in the grouping of objects displayed in current books is in fact a recognition of the greater concreteness of such objects.

In the second place, the prior introduction of sets and additional explicit notation permits mathematically exact and precise definitions and concepts rather than the often vague and ambiguous notions encountered in explanations of relations between concrete groups of objects and the Arabic numerals. For example, students can learn a clear, simple and meaningful characterization of numbers as properties of sets. Children who have learned the notion of a property can learn that a precise answer to the question, "What is a number?" is, "A number is a property of a set." Continual emphasis of this definition of numbers precludes learning number symbols as meaningless symbols or addition as a meaningless operation performed on meaningless number symbols. Numbers are properties of sets and the operation of addition of numbers is simply a general way of combining families of sets of things without paying any real attention to the things themselves.

With this definition *zero* presents no special difficulty and takes on no special mystique but is introduced as the numerical property of the empty set, the set which has no members. Empirical evidence strongly suggests that less difficulty is encountered with zero in arithmetical operations than with any other number when it is introduced as a property of the empty set.

The introduction of explicit notation makes the definition of number clear. Ordinarily, we can only assume understanding of the relationship when we make the great leap in abstraction from groups of objects to numerals which name their particular number properties. The use of set notation allows the steps in abstraction to be made explicit. The first step in abstraction is describing a set in the following way:

The next step in abstraction is the N notation:

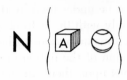

This notation names a number but at the same time it maintains the pictorial character of the set description. In this sense it may be considered a "transition" to the Arabic numerals. Here we have abstracted from the particularity of the objects in the set to the single property of number. We must assume that children understand this step if they are to have any understanding of the way a number is related to a set of objects. The notation makes the step clear and precise in a way not permitted by verbalization at the primary grade level. The final step is to the Arabic numeral which in our example is:

$$2$$

Thus the explicit notation for sets introduces the student at the very beginning of his mathematical experience to the easily comprehended operations on sets—rather than to the more difficult and more abstract operations on numbers. Moreover the introduction of notation for sets permits consideration of addition and subtraction of numbers without commitment to the particular notation of Arabic numerals. The possibility of breaking free from the reiterated use of this single notation for numbers does much to eliminate the tendency to focus on the numerals themselves without consideration of their meaning. To illustrate these points about concreteness and meaningfulness the introduction of addition at three levels is illustrated as follows:

In the first line the concrete operation of putting sets together, that is, of forming their *union*, is indicated. In the second line the notation of N in front of a set is used to indicate the number of objects in the set. This notation permits a very simple transition from the concrete putting together of objects to the abstract use of Arabic numerals, introduced in the third line.

Throughout the beginning materials, set operations are presented as concrete analogues to numerical operations. Union of sets and addition of numbers are presented in sequence, difference of sets and subtraction of numbers are presented in sequence, etc.

Compared to most books, the present program introduces an extensive mathematical vocabulary and notation. It is believed that the use of explicit notation permits a clarity of definition of concepts that is otherwise impossible so that the student can develop a deeper understanding of number concepts. The essential nature of notation for precision in mathematics cannot be overlooked, for it is a truism of the history of mathematics that many strides of major importance have depended almost solely on the introduction of an appropriate mathematical notation. It is indeed difficult to penetrate far in mathematics without the development of an explicit notation.

Experimental work with the material during the academic years, 1959-60 and 1960-61, has shown that primary-grade youngsters do not have any difficulty in grasping new notation (Suppes and McKnight, 1961). As long as the notation introduced is explicit and precise and corresponds to simple notions, no difficulties of comprehension arise. The notation and vocabulary introduced in the program have already been tested and have been found to be well within the capacity of the primary-grade child.

The results of a general achievement test given to 25 experimental and 25 control first grade classes in May 1961 are shown in Table 4 (page 118). This achievement test was constructed by the project staff in order to provide a detailed profile of achievement levels on the standard arithmetical topics. It is important to emphasize, of course, that this test did not include any of the special notation introduced in the Sets and Numbers program, because the same test was administered to both experimental and control groups. This achievement test was used rather than one of the standard achievement tests like the Metropolitan because we wanted to get a more detailed picture of achievement levels.

Similar results were obtained in the spring of 1962 with the arithmetic portions of the Metropolitan Achievement Tests, but I shall not cite the numerical data here.

Finally let me state that we have also conducted an experimental pedagogical program in the teaching of mathematical logic to selected fifth- and sixth-grade students. The project was conducted as a demonstration project under the sponsorship of the Office of Education. The purpose of the project was to introduce the academically able elementary school child to modern mathematics and mathematical methods at a level which is completely rigorous and simple enough in presentation and context to permit relatively easy comprehension. We are particularly interested in the capacity of children in the fifth- and sixth-grade age levels to

Table 4. Sets and Numbers Project
Results of General Achievement Tests, First Grade Classes, May 1961[*]

Possible Total Score 118

	N of Students	N of Classes	Mean	Median
Experimental Group	595	25	97.39	104
Control Group	539	25	86.68	90

Difference of means
Significant P < .01

Comparison of Groups on Item Type

		Proportion of Correct Answers to Total Possible Per Type of Item	
Items		Experimental Group	Control Group
1-4	Recognition of groups	.99	.99
5-6	Recognition of numerals	.99	.99
7-10	Writing numerals	.98	.97
11-22	Sequence of numerals	.95	.93
23-25	Telling time	.97	.97
26	Fractional part—half	.93	.92
27-29	Ordinals	.94	.94
30-35	Decimal system of numeration	.99	.97
36-43	Column addition	.94	.90
44-51	Column subtraction	.86	.79
52-54	Addition—2 digit numbers	.69	.50
55-59	Addition of 3 numbers	.65	.30
60-67	Column addition and subtraction	.67	.55
68-79	Addition and subtraction— equations	.85	.55
80-95	Equations—fill in blanks	.80	.75
96-105	Complex equations	.61	.41
106-112	Multiplication—additive	.72	.65
113-118	Operation symbols	.84	.77

[*] Tests were administered by classroom teachers in all classes, experimental and control.

do the kinds of deductive proofs which are characteristic of modern mathematics and to examine the possible transfer of skills of analysis and correct reasoning to other subject matter areas. In connection with this pedagogical program we have also conducted a number of experiments on the grasp of principles of logical inference and the learning of the beginning elements of mathematical logic from a learning-theoretic standpoint, but I do not have the space nor the time here to report in detail on these experiments. We hope to be able to make such reports generally available in the future (for a preliminary report, see Suppes, 1962).

References

C. J. Burke, W. K. Estes and S. Hellyer. "Rate of Verbal Conditioning in Relation to Stimulus Variability." *Journal of Experimental Psychology* 48: 153-61; 1954.

C. L. Hull and K. W. Spence. " 'Correction' vs. 'Non-correction' Method of Trial-and-Error Learning in Rats." *Journal of Comparative Psychology* 25: 127-45; 1938.

J. V. Murphy and R. E. Miller. "The Effect of Spatial Contiguity of Cue and Reward in the Object-Quality Learning of Rhesus Monkeys." *Journal of Comparative Physiological Psychology* 48: 221-29; 1955.

J. V. Murphy and R. E. Miller. "Spatial Contiguity of Cue, Reward and Response in Discrimination Learning by Children." *Journal of Experimental Psychology* 58: 485-89; 1959.

E. Stoll. "Geometric Concept Formation in Kindergarten Children." Ph.D. dissertation, unpublished, Stanford University, 1962.

P. Suppes. "Mathematical Logic for the Schools." *The Arithmetic Teacher* 9: 396-99; 1962.

P. Suppes and R. Ginsberg. "Experimental Studies of Mathematical Concept Formation in Young Children." *Science Education* 46: 230-40; 1962a.

P. Suppes and R. Ginsberg. "Application of a Stimulus Sampling Model to Children's Concept Formation With and Without an Overt Correction Response." *Journal of Experimental Psychology* 63: 330-36; 1962b.

P. Suppes and R. Ginsberg. "A Fundamental Property of All-or-None Models, Binomial Distribution of Responses Prior to Conditioning, with Application to Concept Formation in Children." *Psychological Review* 70: 139-61; 1963.

P. Suppes and Blair A. McKnight. "Sets and Numbers in Grade One, 1959-60." *The Arithmetic Teacher* 8: 287-90; 1961.